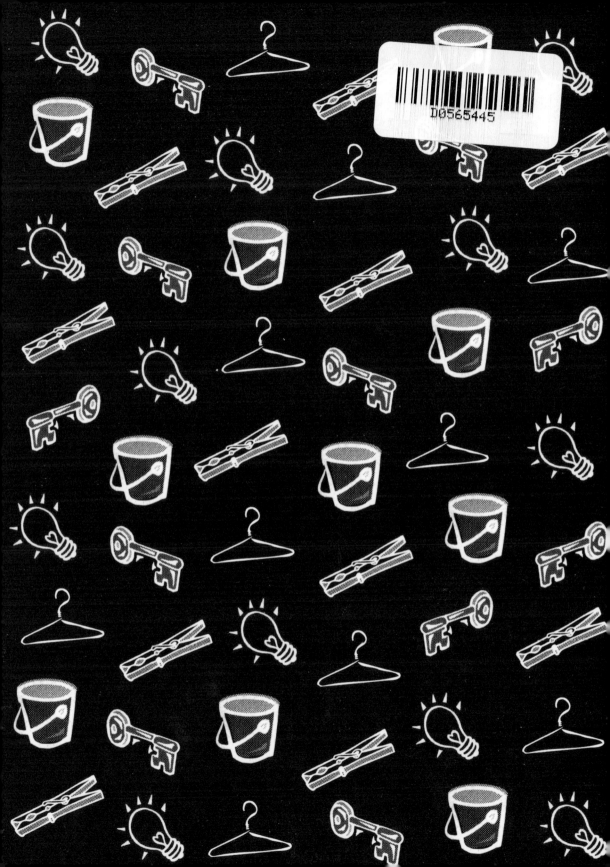

good house magic

good house magic

back-to-basics
Housekeeping
in a flash

natalia marshall

MQP

Published by **MQ Publications Limited**
12 The Ivories
6-8 Northampton Street
London N1 2HY
Tel: +44 (0)20 7359 2244
Fax: +44 (0)20 7359 1616
email: mail@mqpublications.com
website: www.mqpublications.com

ISBN: 1 84072 451 X

1 3 5 7 9 0 8 6 4 2

Printed and bound in China

Contents

Contemporary householders have access to all kinds of labor-saving gizmos. Running a home successfully and efficiently still relies to a great degree on common sense, however, and a little elbow grease. Our house-proud mothers' and grandmothers' generations did an awful lot of scrubbing, mopping, heaving, and squeezing, which thankfully we no longer have to do. But maybe we have come too far the other way. There is perhaps a tendency to rely too heavily on energy-guzzling machines to do the heavy stuff, and powerful chemicals to clean and sanitize when it's not strictly necessary. If we're not careful, we may end living in sealed, sterile boxes that are ultimately unhealthy.

No one wants to go back to the dark ages of domestic slavery when doing the washing took an entire day, but being a responsible householder today should entail using resources responsibly and economically, and going easy on the chemicals. We need to conserve energy and reduce pollution for the generations

Put the Magic back into Household Chores

to come. This doesn't need to be a hardship, though. The good news is that new technology is helping to make electrical appliances, such as vacuum cleaners and washing machines, more sophisticated. Cleaning aids are increasingly being made with environmentally-friendly substances, such as fruit acids, that clean just as well as more toxic materials. Thank goodness for cyclical trends, too, which mean that it's now perfectly acceptable to salvage some of the wise housekeeping ideas of "the olden days"; going retro has never been so cool.

It's said that the most important commodity of the twenty-first century is time, so maybe we all need to slow down a little and pay more attention to our immediate surroundings. A little nurturing goes a long way, and it's rather comforting to stop, take stock, and allow oneself the luxury of sparing a few hours a week tending to the place where most of us spend the majority of our time. Great home style is accessible to everyone—there are endless TV programs and magazines devoted to home interiors, and the shops are bulging with beautiful furnishings, fabrics, and accessories from all over the world that have become seductively affordable. These gorgeous trappings deserve a worthy backdrop.

Having a lovely, home, then, is all about blending the common sense and dislike of waste of days gone by with the very best that modern technology has to offer. This book is full of easy-to-follow advice and magic tips that will work wonders for anyone who takes pride in their home and wants to make it clean, orderly, and of course, beautiful. We've given you the basics, to which you can add your own special methods that work best for your home: pester your grandma for her favorite housekeeping secrets; hunt around in secondhand bookstores for old books that outline traditional home maintenance methods; go online and trawl the web for the astonishing amount of practical information that is shared globally; quiz canny (and houseproud) friends about their habits. In time, you'll build up a store of amazing knowledge that you can annotate and keep, passing it on to others just as others passed on their wisdom to you.

chapter **1**

Setting up your Home

Let's Get Started

Getting your home to run efficiently frees you to spend more time doing the things you enjoy. Everyone has their own systems, and if you can persuade all members of the household to join in, you'll soon have a home that runs smoothly.

■ Set aside a regular time each week to deal with correspondence and bills and to plan your chores and appointments for the week ahead.

■ Organize a simple filing system for your important paperwork so that you can access documents easily when you need them, and make use of your home computer (if you have one) for doing household accounts.

■ Think about ordering your grocery shopping online. Setting this up can be a hassle, but once your supermarket has your master list of preferred items, it saves huge amounts of time at a very reasonable cost.

Lists

Making lists may not rate highly as a thrilling way to pass the time, but they really do make your life easier and enable you to use your time more efficiently. Some of the most useful lists include:

■ All food and household items that you shop for regularly. Stick it on your fridge door, and add to it as necessary.

■ Dates of birthdays, perhaps on a large calendar, with social events, holidays, and appointments. All members of the family can transcribe their plans onto the calendar.

■ Tasks for the week.

■ Vacation preparation.

■ Parties, including dinner parties and other social gatherings.

De clutter your home

Piles of clutter are unsightly, take up too much room, and make keeping track of things a nightmare. It is really worth the effort to sort through your belongings regularly and throw out unwanted items. Recycle as much as possible (see page 88 for more about recycling), or donate items to charity. It may

be helpful to allocate to each member of the family a named shelf for storing items used frequently, to save time hunting around. Make use of dead space such as alcoves, behind doors, and under stairs to house storage boxes of all shapes and sizes. Labeling everything will make life even easier.

Create a home record book

It's incredibly useful to have a mastersource of information about your home. You can put together a home record book manually, in a ring binder for instance, or on your home computer. Keep your record in a sensible place where it is readily to hand, and make sure that all members of the household know where it is kept. Some of the key items to include are:

■ **Essential telephone numbers**
Keep a list of emergency telephone numbers and a health section with details of every visit made to a doctor by a family member. A

section for local services such as taxis, good restaurants, swimming pools, and libraries is also useful.

■ **Renovation and maintenance**
Write down the names, addresses, and telephone numbers of anyone you've used for repairs, renovating, or decorating, plus details about what repairs were done and when. List also good products you have used yourself, and how you dealt with any spills or stains.

■ **Household diary**
Keep a list of dates such as birthdays, school terms, inoculations, and dates when bills, such as insurance, have to be paid. Update it each year, transfering the dates to a calendar.

■ **Household inventory**
Make a complete list of your most important possessions, with photos if necessary, in case you suffer from fire or burglary. (For more advice on caring for special things, see page 67.) File guarantees, instruction leaflets, and the dates of purchase of major items.

■ **Entertaining**
If you often entertain, make a record of the guests you invited to each event and the food that was served. Keep a record of other hosts to whom you owe invitations.

■ **Gardening**
Keen gardeners can set up gardening records that contain essential planting details.

■ **Car**
Set up a car file with details such as insurance policies and dates of repairs.

■ **Cleaning**
Keep a cleaning file to record any special treatments you've used, including successes with tricky stain removal.

She hasn't time to worry!

Turn a House into a Home!

Your personal touches make your home unique and welcoming, and a carefully considered interior scheme contributes enormously to a sense of cohesion. It's much easier to think about how you want your home to look and feel before you move in, but of course you can continue to develop and evolve the ambience over many years.

Using color

The way you decorate and use color is the key to creating the kind of mood you feel comfortable with in your home. There are various approaches: a complementary scheme, for example, uses colors that harmonize with each other; contrasting schemes use color opposites, and these tend to be more dramatic. Before you reach for the paint samples, think about what the room will be used for and what atmosphere you want to create—do you want a calm and relaxing mood or one that is bright and energizing?

If you want your room to feel light and airy, choose soft, pale, and complementary colors. For a cozy atmosphere select warmer tones such as deep apricots, terracotta, and mustards. For impact, rich tones and contrasting schemes are the right choice.

North-facing rooms can look quite somber, so use warm colors to compensate. In south-facing rooms where daylight streams in all day, you can afford to experiment with cool colors like pale greens and blues. Window size and the color and density of your window treatments can also affect the amount of daylight that enters your rooms.

In rooms that are mainly used in the evenings, artificial light will brighten any gloomy spots and create an impression of more space. Be sure to check your chosen color sample in both natural and artificial light, as colors can vary dramatically. You should also take noteworthy architectural features, such as fireplaces, picture rails, coving, or ceiling roses, into consideration.

Having a completely empty room as a starting point is a luxury that few of us enjoy. Usually you have to work with existing carpets, curtains, furniture, and fittings. You may want to match the main color of your fabric or carpet with a paint swatch and then look at using both complementary and contrasting colors for decorating.

Color can be used to correct strange room proportions.

- Light colors visually push walls away while dark tones pull them in.
- Deep color used on a high ceiling will help make it seem lower and the room more cozy.
- Paint end walls darker than the main walls. This will make them appear to "advance," so that a narrow room will look wider and more spacious.

Make a storyboard

Take a tip from professional stylists and put together a storyboard. You can make it from a large piece of white cardboard, sticking down samples of paint colors, fabrics, and flooring, and magazine features that appeal to you. Put large samples on big areas, such as walls, and smaller samples for your accessories to give you a fairly balanced idea of how your scheme will look.

The color wheel is a useful tool for deciding on color schemes and a foolproof way of choosing complementary or contrasting colors. Complementary colors are next to each other on the color wheel whereas contrasting ones are opposite.

Brighten up your Lighting Ideas

Overhauling your lighting is the single most effective way of enlivening your decor. To come up with a workable lighting scheme, think about how you use each room, and the mood you want to create. You'll need a source of overall lighting, which should be neutral and low-key, ideally from more than one point. You can then highlight objects on walls and shelves, or create a pool of light on the floor or for a specific task. Different rooms obviously have different needs.

In **kitchens** you need functional lighting. Recessed halogen ceiling lights or up-lighters provide a bright, natural-looking background light; strip lighting or halogen lights under units provide well-lit worktops; and spotlights can highlight a favorite feature.

Dining areas or rooms benefit from a softer light. A warm downlight low over the table will create intimacy. Sidelights, or a table or standing lamp, also provide a cozy dining atmosphere. Don't make it so dark that your guests can't see what they're eating!

In **bedrooms** warm, soft sidelights can be complemented by brighter lights for the dressing table, wardrobes, and around the bed for reading.

Bathrooms should focus light on water, glass, and mirrors, and create a sense of color and space with spotlights.

When it comes to **workrooms**, natural-style white halogen lighting is less stressful on the eyes. If you work on a computer, overhead lighting should illuminate your keyboard without producing glare and screen reflection. Desk lamps should be angled away from the screen.

In **living rooms** plan the lighting as a series of layers. You'll need a subtle main light, probably with a dimmer switch, supplemented with other light points, for example an adjustable lamp with a halogen bulb behind the sofa for reading. Uplighting, either on the wall or an uplighter, or table lamps, soften the lighting in a room and are good to use instead of a harsh main light. Cabinets with glass doors can be dramatically enhanced with lighting, perhaps by small halogen lights, or you could try highlighting a chimneybreast, favorite painting, or ornament with a spotlight or two. Walkover halogen lights can be recessed at floor level for a subtle contemporary light, or tilted slightly against a wall.

For **halls**, **landings**, **and stairs** where lights may be on for long periods, you can be friendly to the environment by using long-lasting energy-saving bulbs. Wall or ceiling fittings are very practical in the hall, often a very busy thoroughfare, and moving lighting out of harm's way is a practical and attractive solution. A bright pool of light on the floor at the end of a hallway draws the eye and provides a welcoming effect. Stairs require good, even lighting, ideally brighter than the hallway below, but spotlights aren't a good choice because they can cause shadows. If you're worried about seeing your stairs, you can buy stair lights that attach to the carpet.

When it comes to **outdoor lighting**, the garden and patio should be treated as extra rooms and lit accordingly. Paths, porches, and steps need good illumination for safety reasons but also can look fantastic if tastefully illuminated. It's nice to play around with mood-enhancing lighting. For patios the ideal combination is a floodlight for visibility, along with decorative lighting for effects and atmosphere. Introduce a string of colored lights in a tree, a spotlight beaming onto an ornamental feature, or carefully placed floodlighting to illuminate a table and barbecue. Large candles that stick into the earth provide a soft light that flickers beautifully in a warm breeze on a summer evening.

It's Easy to be a Kitchen Genius

Being able to move seamlessly around the kitchen, between fridge, cooker, and store cupboard, grabbing pots, plates, and utensils, is a joy. Just a few tips and tricks can make your experience in the kitchen both enjoyable and efficient.

Kitchen planning

The most important part of creating a new kitchen is the planning. What shape will the kitchen have, how many people will use it, and how often?

You'll need to decide whether to install a fitted or freestanding kitchen. If you choose a fitted kitchen, you will make the most of your space, since all the difficult corners can be hidden and used for storage. You can choose flat pack, rigid, or custom-built to suit your needs and budget. A fitted kitchen will also

add value to your home, but you can't take it with you when you move.

You may, however, prefer the more informal look of a freestanding or non-fitted kitchen, where you can mix different units together to suit your needs. When you move you can take your furniture with you without a problem and use it again.

Kitchen planning tips

■ Plan your kitchen according to your lifestyle. A family will have different expectations of a kitchen than a young couple.

■ Keep the existing service points in mind when planning the kitchen because rewiring and replumbing takes a lot of time and money if you don't get it right first time.

■ Think about the ventilation points—don't plan cupboards over them.

■ Decide where your sink, dish rack, and dishwasher need to go first because this will be the biggest unit to fit in. Take piping, especially waste pipes, into account because they may need an external wall near by.

■ Plan the main areas (sink, food preparation, and hob) close together for greater efficiency.

■ It helps if you know the exact shape of the walls when measuring the size of the kitchen, if there is an inward corner in the room, for instance, it will influence the worktop shape and the position of the wall-cupboards.

■ In a small and narrow kitchen you can maximize space by making the wall-cupboards tall and slim rather than having them protruding outward.

■ Store heavy items in the cupboards underneath the worktop rather than on high shelves so that nothing heavy can fall on your head and you can lift and move them easily.

■ Store items that are rarely used on the highest shelves of cupboards to keep accessible space for items used daily. Make sure cookbooks are within easy reach.

■ Kitchen drawers inevitably end up crammed full of bits and pieces such as pens, coins, and matches. Use little plastic boxes or special drawer organizers for speedy access.

■ Store your utensils near to where you are most likely to use them. This will make your kitchen more efficient.

■ Keep your worktop free from clutter for a tidy, streamlined look.

■ Try to integrate your main waste receptacle into the area below the worktop and right by the food preparation area.

Kitchen essentials

There are all kinds of gadgets for modern cooks but some of them save more labor than others. Aside from the major appliances, such as a fridge and washing machine, try to equip your kitchen with a selection of the cooking aids listed in the chart on page 19. Choose the best quality you can afford and don't be tempted to buy aesthetically pleasing, but nonessential extras if your kitchen is quite small and can't fit them all in.

BUILD YOUR OWN SET OF ESSENTIAL...

Kitchen Tools

Hamburger Turner

Mixing Spoon

Potato Masher

Soup Ladle

Yours Free

4-PLACE KITCHEN WALL RACK

Cooking Aids

Knives of varying sizes

Vegetable peeler

Four-sided grater

Lemon zester

Mortar and pestle

Salt and pepper mills

Lemon squeezer

Sieves

Flour/sugar dredger

Colander

Spoons: wooden, draining,
   and serving

Large forks: metal and wooden

Balloon whisk

Spatulas

Fish slice

Kitchen and pasta tongs

Scales

Measuring cup,
   measuring spoons

Oven and sugar
   thermometers

Garlic press

Apple corer

Ice-cream scoop

Metal skewers

Saucepans & Casseroles

Saucepans: available in a
   variety of sizes with long,
   stay-cool handles, and lids

Cast-iron griddle

Casseroles with lids,
   especially oven-to-table kinds

Steamers

Wok

Electrical Gadgets

Hand whisk

Multipurpose food processor
   (can be the compact kind)

Blender

Toasted-sandwich maker

Baking Equipment

Rolling pin

Pastry brushes

Pastry cutters

Cake and loaf tins

Tart and pie tin

Cookie sheets

Cooling rack

...and things you can live without

Potato ricer *(use a hand whisk instead)*

Ice-cream maker *(unless you have a large family)*

Deep-fat fryer *(unhealthy and cumbersome)*

Slow cooker *(use oven at low
   temperature instead)*

Pasta machine *(unless you live on fresh pasta)*

Salad spinner *(use a colander)*

Ceramic baking beans *(use any dried beans)*

Piping sets *(strictly for baking fiends)*

Asparagus steamer *(use a standard steamer)*

Fish kettle *(wrap your fish in foil and oven bake)*

Bread-making machine
   (strictly for dedicated bread lovers)

Blowtorch
   (unless you can't live without crème brûlée)

Espresso coffee machine *(costs a fortune)*

Making the Best of your Bathroom

The bathroom may be one of the smallest rooms in the house, but it's one where you're likely to spend many a happy hour sluicing, preening, scrubbing, relaxing, and splashing, so it's wise to choose surfaces, sanitaryware and accessories that are easy to keep pristine and gleaming—as well as beautiful—especially if you live in an area of hard water that leaves limescale deposits.

If you live alone you have no one but yourself to please when it comes to designing the bathroom. But family bathrooms need to suit the needs of every member of the household and this can be quite a challenge with an average-sized room. With plenty of organization and storage space, however, everyone can be accommodated. Bathroom schemes work best when the bathtub, basin, and toilet are all white. White-painted rooms can be stark, though, so experiment with warm or bright colors to breathe life and character into the room. You can also be inventive with the lighting, focusing on water, glass, and mirrors, or creating a sense of color and space using spotlights.

Draw a scale floor plan on squared paper. Sketch the bath, basin, toilet, and any other units, such as towel rack or shelving, that you wish to include on pieces of cardboard or paper that can be moved around. Keep experimenting with different combinations until you devise a workable layout.

Before you go shopping for a bathroom suite, decide on your budget. Find out exactly what is included in any quotations—faucets, bath panels, and handrails may cost extra.

Which bathtub?

You'll need a tub that suits the needs of you and your family. If space is a problem, many manufacturers now make special space-saver ranges that include basins and toilets that fit into corners and bathtubs with tapered ends that fit into rooms that have an awkward shape. Different bath panel designs add the finishing touch to your new bath and will complement the style of your room. For a mellow, informal look you could choose pine. For a more traditional style select elegant mahogany-effect panels. Unfinished wood panels can be painted, stained, or wood-washed in the color and finish of your choice. Or you could choose a hardboard panel, finished off with tiles or tongue-and-groove cladding.

Acrylic bathtubs: these are lightweight, warm to the touch, and fairly affordable. Acrylic bathtubs are not rigid, so they can creak or distort slightly when you climb in.

a quick bath in the old home

They are prone to scratches, so avoid abrasive cleaners and bleach. Acrylic bathtubs come in different colors, are often molded into interesting shapes, and can include handrails.

Enameled steel bathtubs: porcelain or vitreous enameled steel tubs are extremely tough, easy to wipe clean, and are available in a range of colors. However, they are quite cold to lean against and tend to be more expensive than acrylic bathtubs, although they should look good for longer.

Corner bathtubs: these take up a little more floor space but can leave valuable wall space for a sink, shower cubicle, or cupboard and may be a good choice for a room with an awkward shape. Some designs incorporate a seat, and many are large enough for more than one bather!

Rolltop bathtubs: these old-fashioned freestanding bathtubs are great for adding a touch of period style to your bathroom and can often be painted to match your bathroom. They usually sit on small ball-and-claw feet. This raises the tub off the floor and so is good for making the bathroom seem bigger. Reproduction fiberglass rolltop bathtubs are

more readily available and affordable than the original cast-iron models. Positioning it in the center of your bathroom may bump up your plumbing costs and the pipes may be visible.
Whirlpool bathtubs: for a touch of luxury you may choose to invest in a whirlpool spa, also known as a spa or Jacuzzi. Small nozzles set in the side of the bathtub pump out water under pressure when the tub is full. Whirlpool bathtubs are very relaxing as the movement of the water massages the body, but they are more expensive than the average bathtub and usually need to be professionally installed.

Basins and faucets

Most freestanding and wall-hung basins are made from vitreous china. This is a type of clay that is fired at a high temperature then glazed to give it a resilient seal. It's tough but can crack, so be careful not to drop heavy objects in the basin.

Basins are normally supported on a pedestal, which also hides the piping. Wall-hung basins are stylish and create an illusion of space, but they are heavy and must be fixed to a solid wall. They can also be semi-recessed into a vanity unit, which provides extra storage space. Corner basins are handy when space is tight, because you can run pipes through adjacent walls or box them off.

Getting extra light

If your bathroom is dark and dingy, try a few of these simple but magic tricks to maximize the light available.
■ Paint the floorboards white or fit a light-colored carpet to reflect light into the room.

■ Fit a large mirror onto a wall or into an alcove. It will make the room look more spacious and reflect light.
■ Tile your bathroom walls white.
■ Use satin or gloss rather than matte paint for a light-reflective finish.
■ Swap curtains for voiles or slatted blinds.
■ Replace ordinary bulbs with halogen bulbs, providing a natural-looking light ideal for shaving or putting on makeup.

Showers

Showers are more economical than baths, and are an invigorating way of getting clean. The type of shower you choose may depend on the way the hot water is already heated in your house—some showers can't be used with some heating systems.
Electric showers can be used within any domestic water system and are normally connected to the mains cold water; an element within the shower heats the water as it passes through the unit.
Mixer showers mix the existing hot and cold water, in a special valve, before it goes to the shower head. A mixer shower will not increase the flow of water to your system, so if your water flows from your faucets slowly, this is the rate at which it will feed the shower.
A **thermostatic mixer shower** incorporates a pre-set thermostat that will sense a dramatic change in temperature and rectify the situation for you.
Power showers are mixer showers with integral pumps that increase the rate of flow from the shower head. They can be installed only in low-pressure, tank-fed systems.

Have a Nice Day at the Office!

An increasing number of people are working from home at least part of the time, and many households have some kind of computer. So setting aside a room or part of a room for a home office makes sense. Even the smallest of spaces can be adapted to accommodate a working area—the corner of a room, an alcove, or even space under the stairs can be adequate. A spare room can be ingeniously designed to fulfill two purposes: a practical working space and a spare bedroom.

Are you sitting comfortably?

Being employed in a professional office often means you have access to ergonomic consultants, but working at home you must take on the role yourself. It's easy to forget how vital it is to have proper office furniture when working at home. Follow these tips to protect your back and prevent the pain of repetitive strain injury.

- Invest in a good chair. It should be adjustable, give plenty of support, and be comfortable to sit on. Your eyes should be level with the middle of your screen.
- Plan your desk. It should have plenty of storage space, be large enough, and be the right height to work at.
- If possible, place your desk by a window to take advantage of the natural light. You'll need to face the window, though, because sunlight will make it difficult to see what's on the computer screen and could strain your eyes. Further protect your eyes with good lighting from main lights or desk lamps.
- Your legs should fit comfortably under the desk, with your feet resting flat on the floor and your knees slightly below hip level
- Your elbows should bend at a 90-degree angle when your hands rest on top of the desk; armrests will provide support.

Planning your office space

A wide range of stylish office furnishings and accessories are available today so it's easier than ever before to create a functional yet good-looking workspace. Make the most of all available space by opting for tall storage units, for example, and slim blinds that can also help cut out the glare of the sun against your computer screen.

Fit sturdy shelving and cupboards and free up desk space by storing essential equipment such as a printer, scanner, and answering machine on a separate shelved trolley.

Neatly and safely hide away dangling cables and wires and don't be tempted to overfill bookshelves. Pens and pencils can be kept tidily in handy pots while stationery and paperwork should be logically organized between trays and your filing cabinet.

Sleek office furniture in metal and glass encourages lots of light into the space, while traditional wooden furniture, whether antique or restored, creates a warmer atmosphere.

Bear in mind that any kind of home office is likely to generate an awful lot of electricity. It's almost certain to have one computer at the very least, possibly two, plus other useful accessories such as a telephone, fax, scanner, printer, modem, CD player, speakers, and

lamps. This type of equipment emits a considerable amount of static, which attracts dust, and also tends to have sensitive surfaces that smear easily, so it should ideally be housed in a place safely out of bounds for children and pets. The home office should be kept dust free as far as possible, with equipment well off the floor, which should itself be easily washable and preferably a hard surface that can be damp cleaned. Don't be tempted to give everything a quick swipe over with a damp cloth—you need special cleaners to maintain the optimum performance of your electricals (see page 38).

Fantastic Flooring

Flooring anchors a scheme, and accentuates the function, mood, and style of a room. The planning of flooring should not be done in isolation. For space to flow naturally in a home, floor coverings need to be coordinated, at least in color. Where different textures or colors meet at doorways, the effect is neater and more hardwearing if a threshold strip is inserted between the two.

Carpets

For some rooms nothing beats a vast expanse of wool. Smarter manufacturing methods have dramatically improved the appearance and durability of even the cheapest carpet. It makes sense to buy better-quality carpets for heavy-wear areas such as living rooms, hallways, and stairs. Bedrooms, bathrooms, and areas of low wear can be fitted with lighter weights to maximize your budget.

Brick

Comparable in price with a good wood or ceramic-tile floor, bricks maintain a comfortable temperature yet are cool in summer.

Floor tiles

Nonslip ceramic tiles can look decorative and are smooth to walk on, albeit cold. Though easily scratched, terracotta tiles retain heat and develop an attractive patina.

"I want flooring that's going to last"

Unglazed quarry tiles

These can be tough, dense, and nonslip, but are somewhat absorbent. Glazed quarry tiles are more resilient. Inlaid with a pattern, encaustic tiles have a soft, matte look. Smaller than other tiles, they are popular in period and historic homes.

Stone floors

Slabs or tiles offer elegance and a timeless quality. They last practically for ever but are cold underfoot and heavy.

Concrete

Resistant to heat and cold, concrete is scratchproof and reasonably priced. It makes a good-looking floor in tile form if painted, stained, or waxed.

Wood

Softwoods and hardwoods are both used for floors. If you choose hardwood, ensure it comes from ecologically managed sources. Consider reclaimed beams and boards, too.

Laminate

Laminate flooring is made from paper printed with a photographic image, usually of wood, glued onto a cheap backing such as MDF (medium-density fiberboard) or hardboard and sealed with a synthetic resin finish. It's affordable and easy to lay yourself, and no trouble to maintain and clean, but does not wear as well as real wood.

Linoleum

Made from natural materials such as linseed

oil and burlap [hessian], modern linoleum is nonslip, burnresistant, and reasonably priced. New production methods mean a great choice of colors and patterns.

Cork

Durable and economical, cork provides a warm, soft, and quiet type of flooring. It is especially suitable in bathrooms, playrooms, kitchens, and hallways.

Vinyl

Vinyl flooring is comfortable to walk on, reasonable in price, easy to clean, and available today in a huge range of colors and designs.

Rubber

Highly durable, soft, warm, and quiet underfoot, rubber is resistant to burns and dents, and comes in bright colors.

chapter 2

Cleaning and Revitalizing

A New Way to Clean

Housecleaning is undoubtedly a tedious chore, but there's always satisfaction to be extracted from a job well done, and pleasure from an orderly, fragrant home. Everyone has an individual way of cleaning. A methodical approach definitely saves time, however, and makes the whole process more efficient. These days there is, if anything, a tendency to overclean. After all, we were not designed to exist in a sterile environment, and modern research shows that exposure to bugs actually improves our immune system's ability to fight off certain illnesses. So be sparing with strong bleaches, cleaners, air fresheners, and disinfectants, and think about experimenting with more natural, safer alternatives. If you do use chemicals, always wear rubber gloves to prevent them from leaching into your skin. For more information about cleaning see also Caring for Special Things on page 67.

Basic cleaning kit

Keep the following items together in an accessible cupboard:

- Half a dozen dusters—you can use old, cut-up cotton T-shirts.
- Polishing cloths made of lint-free cotton.
- Household gloves—use rubber or acrylic as protection against chemicals; fine, disposable gloves for unhygienic cleaning jobs; and cotton gloves for dusting, etc.
- A good dustpan and brush, and long-handled broom.
- Mop and bucket with wringer.
- Nonstick plastic-coated scouring pads.
- Old toothbrushes for cleaning into awkward crevices and corners.
- A selection of cleaning products—especially good are brands that are environmentally friendly.
- Kitchen sponges for wiping surfaces.

A speck of dirt

Household cleaners contain strong chemicals that can harm our bodies and the environment. Research suggests that overusing cleaners and toiletries is partly responsible for the increase in conditions such as asthma and eczema, which occur when our immune systems are damaged. While hygiene is obviously important, especially when it comes to food preparation, there is no need continually to clean all surfaces with antibacterial cleaning solutions—we need some bacteria to help build up immunity. Very often, mild and natural cleaners such as vinegar, bicarbonate of soda, and lemon juice do the job just as well.

Make your own potpourri

It's easy to make your own potpourri to introduce a natural fragrance into your home and you can blend a variety of ingredients to create different moods. Basic ingredients include:

Herbs and leaves: herbs such as rosemary, thyme, and lavender are more fragrant when dried. Other sweet-smelling herbs include mint, myrtle, scented geraniums, sage, lemon balm, bay, and basil.

Going Green
Keep food cupboards insect-free with sprigs of dried, fragrant herbs such as mint, rue, tansy or pennyroyal.

Dried flowers: look for scented flowers such as roses, wallflowers, violets, honeysuckle, lavender, peony, carnations, pinks, and stock. If you want to add more color, choose varieties such as forget-me-not, hydrangeas, marigolds, zinnias, and nasturtiums. Dry them in a cool oven.

Spices: roughly crush (but don't pulverize) dried spices, such as cinnamon, cloves, nutmeg, allspice, anise, coriander seeds, and cardamom. Add whole cloves, pieces of whole mace, or a cinnamon stick.

Fragrant woods and citrus peel: woods that work well in potpourri include sandalwood, sassafras, and cedar. The dried peel of such citrus fruits as oranges, lemons, and limes add color, aroma, and zest.

Essential oils: if you want extra fragrance, add a few drops of pure essential oils according to your taste, but use sparingly so as not to overpower other scents.~

Dealing with odors naturally

Household sprays and air fresheners are among the worst offenders when it comes to overloading our systems—and the environment—with chemicals. Luckily there are many other ways of eliminating unpleasant household smells.

■ Vinegar is an excellent natural deodorizer—a small bowl of vinegar left in any room will neutralize smells. For pervading odors such as those of stale cooking or cigarette smoke, boil a small saucepan of water and vinegar for 15 minutes.

■ A few slices of lemon boiled in water will also work to neutralize odors.

■ Simmer some cloves in boiling water or cook sugar and cinnamon, or vanilla, over a low heat to create a mouthwatering smell of home baking.

■ Burn pinecones or citrus peelings in the fireplace for natural fragrance.

■ Certain houseplants such as flowering begonia, schefflera, peace lily (*spathiphyllum*), spider plant (*chlorophytum*), and Swiss cheese plant (*monstera*) are good for humidifying and oxygenating the atmosphere in your home. They absorb toxins such as carbon monoxide

and VOCs (volatile organic compounds), too.

■ Essential oils are wonderfully aromatic, and good for you too! You can buy essential-oil burners very cheaply. Simply add a few drops of aromatherapy oil to the water dish above the candle burner, but leave it out of the reach of children. Scented candles are good, too—buy the best quality you can afford.

The Household Genie's Tip

Don't throw away old toothbrushes. They are ideal for reaching into tiny crevices or into awkward corners when cleaning. It's a good idea to stick colored tape around the handles to indicate to all members of the family, especially children, that these are not to be used for cleaning teeth. Keep them hidden away to avoid misuse.

Mythbuster!

You don't need to scrub your home with antibacterial solutions—a sterile living environment is not beneficial unless you have specific health problems.

Sparkling Bathrooms

Water and steam on mirrored or porcelain surfaces need extra attention to keep bathrooms sparkling.

Baths

There are lots of good cleaning products for the bathroom but be sure to check that the one you're using is suitable for your type of bathroom fixtures because some products can damage certain bath surfaces. So always read the instructions carefully—it's easier than paying out for a new bath in a year's time. Rinse and dry your bath well to prevent water from forming marks on surfaces. Scale (limescale) can be shifted using lemon juice or white vinegar. Regular cleaning prevents soap and scum build-up, making your job easier.

Acrylic: don't use scourers or abrasive cleaners on acrylic or fiberglass bathtubs; use a sponge and gentle spray cleaner instead.

Enamel: avoid using acid-based cleaners on enameled bathtubs because they eventually erode the surface. Magic away marks with a sponge and liquid detergent. The most stubborn stains can be shifted with mineral (white) spirits rubbed on with a soft cloth.

Fiberglass: use dishwashing liquid and avoid abrasive cleaners.

Mirrors

A soft cloth moistened with a few drops of methyl alcohol will remove most marks from a mirror. You can prevent a mirror from misting over in a steamy bathroom by rubbing a little dishwashing liquid over it and polishing it with a clean cloth.

Going Green
Don't throw your squeezed lemons away. Get into the habit of keeping them in the fridge to wipe over your faucets and porcelain surfaces if scale is a problem in your area.

Showers

Immerse or soak the showerhead in white vinegar to clear chalky scale (limescale) deposits. Use an old toothbrush to clear blocked holes. White vinegar and an old toothbrush can also be used for removing deposits from the shower doors. Nylon shower curtains can be washed in the washing machine with biological detergent to clear soap build-up and get rid of mold. Most other soft materials can be washed by hand in warm water and detergent, then rinsed and drip-dried. If mildew is a problem, clean it off with a paste made of borax and vinegar.

Faucets

Wash faucets using a bathroom cream cleaner then rinse and buff with a soft cloth. Avoid abrasive cleaners and scouring pads as these will scratch the finish. Remove dirt from around the faucets by brushing them with an old toothbrush dipped in cleaner. The acid in lemons can also remove scale (limescale). Rub the faucets with thick slices, leave for a few minutes, and then rinse off. For heavy deposits around the spouts of faucets, fill a small plastic bag or yogurt carton with white vinegar and tie the bag around the spout so that the spout sits in the solution. Leave overnight, remove the bag in the morning, and wipe away any remaining scale. Real chrome faucets can be restored to their original glory with car chrome cleaner. To clean gold-plated faucets, wipe gently with a slightly damp cloth.

Toilets

A daily sluice with a mild disinfectant and a quick brush with a toilet brush is essential to keep toilets clean. Don't leave strong bleach in the toilet bowl for long periods of time because it can cause cracking. If scale (limescale) builds up in the toilet bowl you need to push the water around the U-bend with a toilet brush until the bowl is nearly empty. Then apply scale (limescale) remover or a mixture of laundry borax and white vinegar. Brush vigorously and use an old toothbrush to reach awkward angles. Wipe the toilet seat every week with a mild disinfectant. Always wear rubber gloves to protect yourself from splashes.

Spotless China and Glass

Clean china ornaments or crockery that is not suitable for a dish washer in a bowl of warm, soapy water, placing an old towel at the bottom for protection. Use an old shaving or makeup brush to work into awkward crevices, and a damp cloth dipped in bicarbonate of soda to rub off stains. Rinse well and dry with a soft cloth. Delicate china plates can be stored with a paper plate between each one to prevent chipping.

Crystal stemware

Washing lead crystal in a dishwasher can cause untold damage, so instead wash by hand in warm soapy water. Allow the crystal to dry and then polish it gently with a soft tea towel. Crevices in cut crystal can be cleaned with an old toothbrush and soapy water. Clean the inside of a crystal decanter by swishing around a handful of rice grains mixed with some detergent and warm water.

Glasses

If you're washing glasses by hand, carefully slip them sideways into warm, soapy water so they don't crack. You can line the bottom of the bowl with an old towel for extra protection. Wash the glasses carefully and add a splash of white vinegar to the rinsing water for an extra-shiny finish.

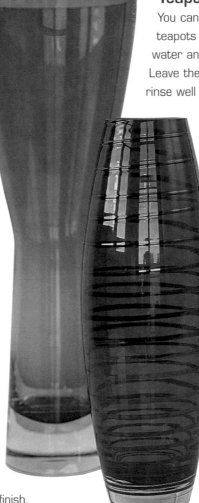

Teapots

You can clean the inside of stained teapots with a solution of warm water and bicarbonate of soda. Leave the solution overnight then rinse well with fresh water in the morning. If you're storing a teapot away, cut the thumb off an unwanted pair of gloves and slip it over the spout so that it doesn't knock against other items and become chipped.

Vases

Clean inside a narrow-necked glass vase by filling it with a mixture of rice or salt and warm water and detergent or white vinegar. Leave this overnight and then rinse. Alternatively, use a long-stemmed bottle brush to gently remove stains and scale.

Looking at China

FOR THE BRIDE

Electrical Equipment

Frequently cleaning and checking the electrical equipment in your home will ensure that it lasts for as long as you need it and stays safe.

Before you start always remember to turn off all electrical appliances. NEVER use wet cloths near plugs or circuits. As you clean check electrical cords for wear and if they need to be changed, follow the manufacturer's instructions. Never yank cords, and make sure that they are kept dry.

To avoid tripping over cords, ensure that they are kept away from main thoroughfares; if they have to be there, make sure that they are covered with tape or a specialist covering to keep them in place. If there is too much wire, coil it loosely and tie it.

Computers

Keeping your computer clean and the vents free of dust helps to maintain your system's performance. Computers generate static electricity, which attracts dust, so they need regular cleaning. It's a good idea to have a special cleaning kit in its own clean bag comprising a soft cloth, an aerosol can of air with a straw-like extension, isopropyl alcohol, cotton swabs, and a CD/DVD drive cleaning kit. When you shut down your computer, the power turns off, but some electrical current still flows through the computer, so to avoid possible injury from electrical shock unplug the power cable and modem line from the wall outlets. Use a damp, lint-free cloth to clean the computer and other parts of your system. Never use abrasive or solvent cleaners that can damage the finish on your components.

Screen: use a soft cloth to clean the screen. Squirt a little water on the cloth (never directly on the screen), and wipe the screen with the cloth. Then wipe it with a damp cloth and fabric conditioner to reduce the static, or use a special antistatic wipe. Take extra care with LCD screens because they are made of specially coated glass and can be scratched or damaged by abrasive or ammonia-based window cleaners.

Keyboard: the easiest way to clean this is to blow dirt from under the keys using an aerosol can of air with a narrow, straw-like extension.

from the mouse ball with a soft cloth. Clean the mouse rollers with a cotton swab dipped in isopropyl alcohol. Replace the mouse ball and clip the retaining ring into place. Always use a clean mouse mat to prevent dust on your desk from damaging the mouse.

Light bulbs

Dirty light bulbs lose efficiency, so keep them clean, especially if they are the energy-saving, long-life variety. Switch off the electricity and allow the bulb to cool if it has been on. Use a well wrung out damp cotton cloth to wipe over it carefully, and wait until it is completely dry before replacing it. Fly spots can be removed with methyl alcohol on a cotton ball.

Telephones

Wipe over telephones regularly using a damp cloth moistened in soapy water then well wrung out, and use a cotton swab dipped in methyl alcohol to clean the handset and dialing pad occasionally. If you're doing something messy, such as painting or gardening, keep a plastic bag by the telephone to put over your hand if you need to answer a call.

Alternatively, turn over the keyboard and shake or tap it gently to release any dust, then use a cotton swab dipped in rubbing alcohol (surgical spirits) or methyl alcohol to clean between the keys. If you spill liquid on the keyboard, turn off the computer and turn the keyboard upside down. Let the liquid drain, then let the keyboard dry before trying to use it again.

Mouse: you can improve the accuracy of your mouse with a thorough clean—it may need it weekly if your computer is in a dusty environment. Turn the mouse upside down and rotate the retaining ring on the bottom of the mouse counterclockwise. Remove the ring and mouse ball. Remove any dust, lint, or dirt

Televisions

Unplug the TV and vacuum all over with the soft brush attachment. Wipe down the screen with a damp, lint-free cloth, and apply an antistatic product if you wish.

Videos and DVDs

Keep the delicate (and expensive) machinery of VCRs and DVDs clean by wiping it over regularly. Use a dust cover if necessary.

Clean Floors in a Flash!

Floors come in for a lot of wear and tear, but even so, often all they need is a vacuum followed by a good mop with warm water and mild detergent.

Brick and stone

Sweep or vacuum a brick or stone floor and then wash it with warm water and a mild detergent.

Carpets

Before shampooing, vacuum thoroughly. If you can, move the furniture out of the room or to one end. Using a carpet shampoo, start at the corner of the room farthest from the door and work back across the room to avoid walking on the damp areas. Allow the carpet to dry thoroughly before replacing furniture—opening the windows will help ventilation. Cut an old plastic bag into pieces and place furniture legs on these to avoid making marks on the carpet. Always test shampoo on an unseen part of the carpet first to check for color fastness. When a heavy piece of furniture has made a dent in

the carpet, you can raise the pile by placing an ice cube in the hollow, leaving it to melt and dry, then vacuuming as normal.

Cork

Mop regularly with warm water and mild detergent and then apply a wax polish.

Linoleum

Marks can be removed from linoleum by scrubbing it with a nonstick scourer and mild detergent or cream cleaner. Use a damp mop and soapy water to clean it thoroughly, then rinse. If you want a shiny finish, use a special emulsion polish.

Marble

Avoid using abrasive cleaners or applicators on marble because it scratches easily. Mop with warm water and a mild detergent, using a blunt knife to lift any stuck-on dirt. The surface can be polished with a silicone wax.

Mats and rugs

Clean cotton bath mats in a washing machine and hang them up to dry. If you can, wait for a warm, sunny day since their bulky texture means they can take a long time to dry thoroughly. Vacuum other mats and rugs regularly to remove grit and dirt that can flatten the pile. If they are not antique or delicate, you could occasionally throw them over the washing line and beat them with a broom. Turn rugs every month or so to ensure that they get even wear. Shampoo rugs in the same way as carpets, but be wary of nonfast vegetable dyes in ethnic-style rugs. Valuable rugs should be cleaned professionally.

Quarry tiles

Glazed quarry tiles should be mopped regularly with warm water and detergent. Unglazed tiles are porous so will absorb dirt easily and must be scrubbed thoroughly (you can buy special tile cleaners for this) then polished with nonslip polish. Faded tiles can be partially restored with steel wool dipped in mineral (white) spirit. You can seal new tiles with linseed oil or a synthetic water-based sealant.

Slate

Wash regularly with soap and detergent then rinse thoroughly. Restore the shine of slate by wiping a little milk over the surface.

Wood

Vacuum out dirt from the gaps between floorboards before cleaning or polishing. Wipe over unvarnished boards with a damp mop and leave them to dry before polishing with a wax floor polish. Buff varnished boards with a nonslip polish. Remove a build-up of solvent-based polish by using medium-grade wire wool and mineral (white) spirit.

Going Green

Sprinkle damp tea leaves or coffee grounds over wooden floors just before sweeping to help collect the dust. To refresh carpets, sprinkle on bicarbonate of soda, leave it for half an hour then vacuum thoroughly. The soda absorbs dirt and odors and discourages dust mites.

Vinyl

Mop vinyl flooring with warm water and detergent then rinse with clean water. Marks can be scrubbed off with emulsion polish.

Dust-Free Furniture!

If you look after wooden furniture well, it should stay beautiful for years. Always dust and polish in the direction of the grain. Some polishes clean and shine at the same time, and most are suited to varnished finishes.

Real wood needs to be cared for, and the best way to protect wooden furniture is with a good-quality wax polish, ideally one containing beeswax. Polish it once a year, perhaps twice a year in cases of heavy use. Apply the wax sparingly with a soft cloth (overuse will cause smearing) then polish the surface with another lint-free cloth. You'll get a good shine from rubbing rather than by using lots of layers of wax. Be wary of using modern silicone sprays on furniture because they can leave a film. If your furniture is pale, avoid using oils, too, as they attract dirt and can darken the wood.

With old or valuable items, it is best to wipe them over with a barely damp cloth dipped in lukewarm water and a mild detergent to remove sticky marks, before polishing with a wax polish.

Here are some tips for taking care with particular types of finish:

French polish: wipe off greasy and sticky marks with a damp cloth then wipe dry immediately.

Oiled wood (such as kitchen worktops): clean with a cloth well wrung out in warm soapy water and rinse. Dry with a lint-free cloth. Reapply your chosen oil when needed.

Painted and varnished finishes: clean painted pieces of furniture with a soft cloth wrung out in warm, soapy water. Rinse with clean water, then wipe dry.

Waxed wood: wipe with a cloth wrung out in warm, soapy water. Wash down any heavily marked pieces and rub particularly bad patches with a nonstick sponge scourer. Rinse and wipe with clean, absorbent cloths to remove all traces of water.

MDF (medium density fiberboard) or laminate: you can keep this clean and dust free by damp dusting with a clean cloth and vacuuming with the soft brush attachment. No polish is needed.

The Household Genie's Tip

You can use a little olive oil and vinegar to polish your furniture. Combine 1 part white vinegar with 3 parts olive oil. Add a little natural lemon oil or other essential oil for extra fragrance. To apply the solution, fill a clean plant spray and mist it over the surface.

Cane and wicker furniture

Cane and wicker furniture needs regular vacuuming to keep the dust out of the small crevices. Lift heavy dirt with fine steel wool dipped in a washing-soda solution (a cupful of soda to a bucket of warm water), or use a soft brush and warm, soapy water. Wipe over with a clean, damp cloth and allow to dry away from direct heat.

To stop wicker furniture from drying out, clean it occasionally with a little vegetable oil on a soft brush. If outside furniture becomes mildewed, you can clean it with a solution of white vinegar or salt and warm water.

Upholstery

Fabric: vacuum fabric-covered upholstery thoroughly (remove stubborn pet hairs and fluff with a piece of adhesive tape wrapped around your hand), then clean off spots and marks. Professional cleaning usually gives the best results, but you can use a foam upholstery shampoo yourself effectively. Test a small patch on a hidden area first.

Loose covers: check the care label inside first and follow the advice. If the covers are machine washable, replace them on the furniture while still slightly damp in case they shrink and to help maintain their shape.

Leather: dust frequently and keep supple with an occasional application of leather cream. Remove grime by wiping over with a damp cloth well wrung out in warm, soapy water.

Lampshades

Brush or vacuum off dust, then spot clean lampshades with dry-clean foam.

FURNITURE
POLISH

A bright
and healthy
home in
every tin

Dazzling Kitchens

Kitchens need more thorough cleaning than most other rooms because of the grime and steam that cooking produces. Also, because all food preparation takes place in the kitchen, it must be an area of good hygiene.

Appliances

Wipe the door fronts and sides of appliances with a cloth dipped in warm water and detergent and wrung out until it is just damp. Appliances will be a little more amenable to moving around for easy cleaning if you rub a little dishwashing liquid in front of their feet before attempting to move them.

Chopping boards

Wooden chopping boards are always best because wood contains its own natural enzymes that destroy bacteria. They can be cleaned with hot, soapy water, then rinsed well. Stains and lingering smells can be banished with lemon juice and a clean plastic nailbrush. Pay special attention if the board has been used for raw meat, and replace a chopping board that is cracked.

Stoves and ovens

Before cleaning, always switch off the power supply to an electric stove. If your oven is the self-cleaning kind, line the bottom with silver foil to accelerate the cleaning process. A watery paste of bicarbonate of soda and water smeared over the oven floor then allowed to dry will absorb grease spatters and is easy to wipe out after cooking. A shallow dish of ammonia left overnight in your oven accelerates the cleaning process, too.

The standard proprietary brands of oven cleaners usually contain sodium hydroxide, which is both toxic and caustic, so look out for the new kind of cleaners now available in most stores that are kinder to skin as well as the environment. If you must use the other kind, follow the manufacturer's instructions very carefully, wear protective gloves, and ensure that the kitchen is well ventilated and that children and pets are out of the way. To avoid using harsh cleaners often, always give the hob a quick wipe after every use, in order to prevent foods from solidifying on the surfaces.

Most burned-on food stains can be easily removed if you wipe over them with a cloth dipped in warm water and detergent then leave for an hour or so before cleaning completely. Pour salt over food spills on the hob and inside the oven to prevent them from burning. Clean up any acidic spills such as fruit or vinegar immediately, especially on enamel surfaces because they can mark.

If you are cooking "ready" meals or a dish that may bubble over place the container on a baking tray to catch spills. Always line grill pans with silver foil that can be thrown away with leftover fats, etc., after use. You can wash dirty oven shelves in the bath if your sink is not big enough, using warm water and biological detergent—but line the bath with old towels first to protect it.

"But isn't one cleaner very much like another?"

Cutlery

Place only dishwasher-proof cutlery in the dishwasher. Silver, bronze, and bone-handled cutlery should always be washed by hand (but not left to soak). Buff cutlery with a soft, clean cloth before putting it away.

Wash silver cutlery as soon as you can after use to stop particles from foods such as egg, fish, broccoli, and salt from tarnishing it. If you have several items of silver or silver-plated cutlery to clean, line the bottom of a plastic bowl with silver foil and place the cutlery on top. Add a handful of washing soda and cover with boiling water to cause an electrochemical reaction to remove the tarnish. Rinse and dry the cutlery thoroughly.

Saucepans know electric cooking is clean

Dishwashers

Wipe over the outside with a cloth dipped in warm, soapy water, and use a special cleaner in an empty wash cycle occasionally for a thorough clean inside. If you live in a hard-water area, make sure that you keep the salt reserve filled up to prevent a build-up of scale. Wipe down rubber seals with lemon juice or white vinegar if scale accumulates.

Extractor fans

Switch off an electric extractor fan before removing the cover to clean the vents. Wipe the hood with a cloth dipped in warm, soapy water. Nonelectric, plastic window fans can be unscrewed and soaked in warm, soapy water to remove dust and grease. Use an old toothbrush to clean grime if neccessary. Rinse and allow it to dry.

Fridges and freezers

Fridges and freezers should be washed out regularly with bicarbonate of soda and warm water. Food should be kept in its original containers so you can check for and throw out food that is past its use-by dates. Freezers and fridges that are not frost free need to be defrosted regularly to keep them working efficiently. Pack food that you want to keep in cold boxes or cardboard boxes lined with newspaper. Turn off the freezer or fridge and take out all the trays to be washed. Use a toothbrush or nailbrush dipped in warm, soapy water to reach into the seals, then rinse and wipe them dry. Use a bowl of hot water to speed up the defrosting process, and a plastic bowl at the bottom to catch the water. You can also line the bottom with an old towel to soak up drips. Wipe inside the appliance with a clean cloth and then replace the shelves and the food.

Irons

Grimy sole plates can be cleaned when warm with bicarbonate of soda rubbed over them with a damp cloth, or simply rub the iron over a damp towel.

Marble worktops

Avoid scratching the surface of marble with abrasive scourers because this can lead to staining. Remove stains by dabbing neat

They live in a lovely fresh home

...because she chooses the safe disinfectant with the freshness of real pines

lemon juice or white-wine vinegar on the mark and then rinse it well immediately.

Microwave ovens

Microwave ovens should be wiped with a damp cloth and the door left open to air them after each use. Soften old spatters of food by bringing a bowl of water to the boil inside .

Pots and pans

Pots and pans are always easier to clean if you soak them first. You can shift persistent smells and some stains by boiling water with a dash of vinegar, and bad burns by soaking for a couple of hours in biological detergent. If you must scrub, plastic-coated scourers are kinder to the surface.

Aluminum: clean using a paste made from equal parts of baking powder, cream of tartar, washing powder, and vinegar. You can remove stubborn marks by boiling natural acid from a lemon, apple peel, rhubarb, or onion in some water for 15 minutes.

Cast iron/woks: clean cast-iron pans build up a tough, dark patina with use, so clean them as little as possible and don't wash them in a dishwasher or leave them soaking for more than 10 minutes. You should mainly clean them with paper towel, and keep them seasoned with a little vegetable oil rubbed onto them with paper towel or a cotton cloth.

Copper: rub the outside with half a lemon dipped in salt to remove tarnish, or fill a spray bottle with vinegar, cover the outside, sprinkle with salt, and then rub clean.

Sinks

Sinks of course, must be kept clean, but avoid harsh abrasive cleaners and bleach as far as possible to keep your sink looking good longer.

Porcelain: this can crack and stain over time. You can use a weak solution of bleach left to soak for an hour, but try baking soda, borax, or vinegar first.

Stainless steel: wash daily with dishwashing liquid. Keep the sink shiny by rubbing with a mix of bicarbonate of soda (or vinegar) and a little warm water.

Chimneys and Fireplaces

Chimney cleaning is usually best left to the professionals, and should be carried out once a year for fireplaces that are in use.

Brick: cleaning out a fire grate can create a lot of dust, so damp down the ashes first using either a plant water mister or some damp coffee grounds or tea leaves. Rub off soot deposits on brick fire backs and surrounds with a wire brush. Use neat malt vinegar to scrub the bricks and then rinse them with clean water.

Cast iron: dampen the ashes and vacuum away dust and soot from the hearth and surround. If you like to apply blacking to burnish the surface, wear rubber gloves and polish the surface with a soft cloth.

Marble: sponge with mild detergent then rinse and dry, or use a specialist product. Soot marks can be removed with lemon juice or white vinegar, but rinse well afterward as the acid can eat into the surface.

Stone: scrub stone fireplaces with a mild bleach solution, rinse thoroughly then dry. Once the surface has dried, protect it from staining with a clear brick and stone sealant.

Make your Metals Shine!

Metals may seem hard and resilient, but in fact some are softer and more prone to damage than you might think, so clean them gently.

Brass and copper

Brass and copper naturally develop a soft patina, which is a plus point on antique items and should not be cleaned off with metal polishes. Instead, buff regularly with a soft cloth or chamois to keep the metals clean, bearing in mind that both metals scratch easily. Heavy staining can be removed with long-term copper or brass cleaners or impregnated wadding, while a light tarnishing can be rubbed off with a long-term silver cloth. Alternatively, mix a level tablespoon of salt with a tablespoon of vinegar in half a pint of hot water and then, using extremely fine steel wool, wipe the brass with the solution without rubbing hard. For copper use a rough cloth rather than steel wool. Wash in hot, soapy water, rinse, dry, and then apply polish.

Wash lacquered brass in warm, soapy water, then rinse it and buff dry. Brass that is not lacquered should be cleaned with proper brass or copper polish—use an old toothbrush to reach fine detailing. A cut lemon dipped in salt is good for removing tarnish. Wash the brass afterward in hot, soapy water. If copper or brass items turn green, you can rub them with a solution of ammonia and salt, but wear gloves. You could also try rubbing them with a paste made of equal parts of salt and flour, moistened with vinegar.

Bronze

Keep bronze items shiny by wiping them with a colorless, neutral shoe polish, or some vegetable oil, and a soft cloth. Alternatively, clean your bronze with salt, vinegar, and flour. Dissolve 1 teaspoon of salt in 1 cup of white vinegar. Add enough flour to make a paste and then apply it to the bronze. Let the paste sit

Going Green
Rust remover—commercial rust removers are highly toxic, but there is a safe homemade alternative. Sprinkle some salt on the rust and squeeze over a lime or lemon until it is soaked. Leave on for two or three hours. Then use the rind to scrub off the rust.

for 15 minutes to an hour before rinsing with clean, warm water. Polish dry.

Stainless steel

Ordinary pans can be washed in the dishwasher, but for kitchen surfaces such as stoves try bicarbonate of soda mixed to a paste with water. Rub over the surface, sponge with warm water and then dry well.

Silver

Silver is a soft metal that is very prone to tarnishing and should be cleaned regularly but carefully. Use a soft cloth and a nonabrasive cleaner because silver is easily damaged, and silver plate can be worn away to the base metal. Embossed, engraved, or raised decoration can accumulate dirt and polish. A soft shaving brush or small paintbrush dipped in polish is useful for reaching difficult areas. To add a quick shine to lightly tarnished silver, rub it over with a paste made from lemon juice and salt. (See also Cutlery on page 46 for cleaning silver cutlery.)

Valuable items should be cleaned professionally. Store silver in a dry place, wrapped in sheets of black or acid-free tissue paper to prevent tarnishing.

Chrome

Use vinegar to clean the chrome in your home. Simply wipe the chrome with a soft cloth that has been dipped in undiluted white, or cider, vinegar. Alternatively, use baby oil on a soft cloth and polish the chrome, removing stains from trim on faucets or kitchen appliances.

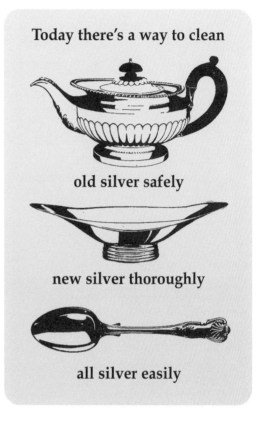

Today there's a way to clean
old silver safely
new silver thoroughly
all silver easily

Gold

Gold is very easy to clean (another reason why it so valuable!). Simply wash it in lukewarm, soapy water and dry with a cotton cloth. Give it a polish using a chamois cloth. Use alcohol or vodka to soak gold in before cleaning, to loosen grease and make washing easier.

Pewter

Dissolve 1 teaspoon of salt in 1 cup of white vinegar. Add enough flour to make a paste, applying the paste to the pewter. Let it sit for 15 minutes to an hour before rinsing with

Outside your House

Don't forget the outside of your home, especially when summer draws to an end, and keep the exterior looking as good as the interior.

The notion of an "outside room" is an established one, and even the tiniest patio, balcony, sun deck, terrace, or yard should be acknowledged as an extension of the home. Outdoor areas exposed to the elements receive a lot more wear and tear than ones indoors—especially if they are south facing—so they need regular attention to keep them from getting grimy, mildewed, moss covered, or

sun bleached. It's usually a case of either giving surfaces a protective coating of some kind, or scrubbing off unwanted deposits; the more you have of the former, the less you'll need of the latter!

Drains

Remove any debris from the cover of a drain and then sprinkle baking soda in the drain opening. Follow this with a cup of white kitchen vinegar. Repeat if neccessary, and finally flush with boiling water.

Patios and furniture

At the end of the summer, clean and put away patio furniture that could be damaged by frost or snow.

Wrought-iron furniture: brush off tree sap and bird droppings, then wash it down with a solution of warm water and detergent. Allow the furniture to dry and then polish it with a silicone wax product.

Wood: wipe over wooden furniture and apply a good wax to unsealed wood, or sand down then varnish any areas that look worn.

Plastic and plastic-coated wire furniture: clean this with a solution of warm water and detergent. Rinse and dry.

Patios: you can buy chemical liquid cleaners, but these are highly toxic, so if you prefer a less harsh method, buy or rent a jet hose whose powerful action lifts dirt and moss.

Gleaming Windows

Windows that face onto busy streets are especially prone to dust and grime, so these—and their curtains and blinds—will need frequent cleaning.

Blinds and shades

Roller blinds: vacuum with the soft brush attachment and if possible sponge with warm water and detergent—you may need to remove them from their fixings to do this (check the instructions for guidance). Rinse well with clean water, then leave to dry thoroughly before rerolling.

Slatted or Venetian blinds: wearing cotton gloves that have been very slightly dampened, wipe with your fingers along each slat, working from the top to the bottom so that dirt doesn't fall on newly cleaned slats.

Curtains

Curtains are expensive to dry-clean, so vacuum them regularly with the soft brush attachment, including valances and pelmets,

at last... "wipe-clean" Venetian blinds!

warm water. You can make your own window cleaner from vinegar and water in an old plant mister. Wipe windows clean with a chamois leather or crumpled newspaper. Don't wash windows on very sunny days because the sun will dry the glass before you have a chance to clean them thoroughly, creating smears. If you're washing outside and inside, use both horizontal strokes on one side and vertical on the other so that you can pinpoint exactly where any smears are.

working from top to bottom with the curtains closed. If you need to take the curtains down for cleaning or washing, mark each inside corner with a permanent marker pen with an R and L for right and left, to remind you which curtain goes on which side.

Vacuum tracks and poles regularly to maintain smooth opening of curtains and to stop dust from falling onto the curtains, and wipe clean occasionally with a damp cloth. Rub soap along the surfaces of tracks and poles to help curtains glide more easily.

Window frames

Painted and varnished frames should only need an occasional wipe over with a damp cloth wrung out in soapy water. Aluminum frames can be rubbed with a paste of borax and water, then rinsed and polished dry.

Window glass

Windows usually need washing inside at least three or four times a year (outside they may need doing once a month) using a mild detergent solution and rinsing with clean,

Tots Spots

Swish Whish

Keeping Walls and Ceilings Looking Good

Walls and ceilings need cleaning just like other parts of the house, especially in kitchens, rooms that are near to traffic-laden streets, or where people smoke. If walls are simply painted with emulsion, a fresh coat of paint will get better results than washing down the surface, which could end up smeared.

Ceramic tiles

Wipe down tiles with warm water and detergent. Use an old nailbrush or toothbrush dipped in white vinegar to clean the grout if it is stained or scaled. You can revive grout by applying a paste of bicarbonate of soda, leaving it for a couple of minutes, rinsing it off and drying with a soft cloth. If it's really grubby, applying new grout will dramtically improve the look of your tiles.

Wall coverings

Contemporary wallpaper is often washable but read the manufacturer's care label if you still have it before you start sluicing with warm, soapy water. If you don't have the label, try a small test patch in an unseen place such as behind a door or under a bed, sponging carefully with warm water and mild detergent. Rinse with clean water by starting from the top of the walls and working to the bottom to prevent streaks from appearing.

Painted walls

If the paint is a satin or eggshell finish, clean stains or other marks first by gently rubbing with a damp cloth and a cream cleaner. Then clean all over with warm, soapy water, working

Going Green

Many household cleaning products, such as furniture polish, oven cleaners, drain cleaners, and air fresheners, are harmful to people and the environment. You can make your own nontoxic cleaners using common household basics like baking soda, vinegar, lemon juice, and salt. The ingredients cost less than commercial cleaners and they do work. Try these:

Bicarbonate of soda: cleans, deodorizes, softens hard water, and acts as a scouring powder.

Washing soda: works as a germ remover and laundry detergent booster.

Vinegar: cuts grease and deodorizes.

Lemon juice: bleaches stains and freshens smells.

Vegetable oil-based liquid soap: cleans almost any surface and acts as a laundry detergent booster.

from the bottom of the walls to the top so any trickles can be quickly mopped up. Change the water regularly in order to prevent streaks from appearing. You might use step ladders to reach and clean the tops of walls, but better still is to use a long-handled sponge-head mop. Rinse from the top to the bottom, and finally clean the skirting. Before you start cleaning, however, think about whether you may end with a better result by simply applying a new coat of paint. With matt emulsion paint it is usually best if you simply paint over the wall with another coat, because if you wash the wall the paint may just come off.

Ceilings

Cover the furniture and carpet then brush or vacuum off cobwebs and dust. Use a foam-headed mop dipped in warm water and mild detergent, squeezing out the dirty water frequently and working backward and forward across the ceiling. Change the water as soon as it begins to get murky to avoid streaks. Finish with clean water and leave to dry. Don't mop near light fittings—use a damp cloth

instead. -1

Getting Rid of Pests

Unwelcome guests of the crawling and flying variety are a nuisance, but before you start putting down strong chemicals, try some traditional remedies first.

Ants: put down chilli powder, talcum powder, borax, dried bay leaves, or lemon peel at the point of entry; squirt lemon juice in holes.

Fleas: sprinkle noniodized salt on carpets; add brewer's yeast or garlic tablets to pets' diet.

Flies and mosquitoes: burn citronella candles; sprinkle a few drops over barbecues. Stand pots of basil, feverfew, or tansy on windowsills. Make your own flypaper with

yellow paper and honey. Don't leave household refuse too near to the house, especially in warm weather; clear away food leftovers from worktops as soon as possible.

Moths: place sachets of cedar chips, dried lavender, or equal parts dried rosemary and dried mint wherever clothes are stored. You can also use cotton balls soaked in essential oil of lavender, cedar, rosemary, or mint.

Mice: dribble peppermint oil on cotton balls and place them around problem locations.

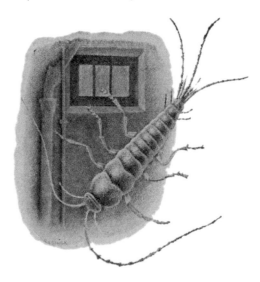

Silverfish and other carpet pests: make a paste of bicarbonate of soda with several drops of lavender and put it in an airtight jar. Leave it for 24 hours to mature and absorb the scent. Sprinkle it on carpets and mats, leave for half an hour, and then vacuum it up.

chapter 3

Stain Removal

Remove the Pain from Stains

These days there are stain removers for all kinds of spills, which increasingly combine newly developed environmentally friendly materials such as fruit acids with great stain-shifting qualities. But you can't always guarantee to have exactly the right specialist product to hand when your pinot noir hits the decks. So here's what to do if disaster strikes and you're caught short—a handful of common household products combine to form the basis for the treatment of most stains. Always try a small, unseen area first, and bear in mind that the stronger the treatment the more likely color is to be removed.

Top tips for stain removal

- Speed is the key to successful stain treatment—act as fast as you can.
- Blot up the excess with paper towel, or scrape it off with a spatula.
- Don't scrub the stain because this will ingrain it further. Instead, dab it gently with a clean, white cloth or a cotton ball.
- Place paper towels or an absorbent white cloth underneath the surface if you can, so that the stain migrates to the material below.
- Test a stain remover on a hidden area first to make sure that it won't damage the fibers or remove the color.
- When using chemical solvents, read the instructions thoroughly and always wear rubber gloves to prevent absorption through your skin.
- Determine what the fabric is made of, because this will affect your choice of treatment. Delicate fabrics such as silk should be professionally dry-cleaned, as should ethnic-style rugs because their vegetable-based colors are often not fast.
- If the stained item is washable, the most effective remedy for biological stains (wine, vomit, food, blood, etc.) is simply to wash immediately with normal biological detergent.
- Protein-based stains on nonwashable surfaces such as milk or blood should be treated with cold, not hot, water.
- Don't dry the stained item before the stain has completely gone, or the stain might set.
- Always wash and rinse the area after the operation to remove any trace of solvent.

The Household Genie's Tip

Always work from the outside in when cleaning a stain to stop it from spreading, and pull the stained area away from anything it touches or backs onto.

Gentle Stain Removers

Commercial stain-removing products can be pricey and won't work on all stains. Try some of these treatments first.

Ammonia

This can get rid of some water-based stains such as wet urine, and is especially good for wool. It's alkaline so it neutralizes acid marks. It gives off unpleasant fumes, though, so use it in a well-ventilated room. It can fade fabrics also so test a small area first. Use diluted 1 part ammonia to 3 parts water.

Bicarbonate of soda (baking soda)

This multipurpose, nontoxic substance cleans, deodorizes, removes stains, and softens fabrics.

Borax (sodium borate)

This natural mineral has been used as a washing aid in households for centuries. It kills mold and bacteria, can be used instead of bleach and is safe on most fabrics. Use a solution of 1 tablespoon (15ml) to 1 pint (500ml) of warm water for sponging or soaking washables. For white cottons sprinkle borax on the dampened stain, stretch the item over a basin and pour hot water through it.

Biological detergent

This contains enzymes that break down organic matter such as blood, urine, milk, etc. If used quickly stains may need no further treatment.

Eucalyptus oil

This oil can remove tar from clothing. It can be bought as essential oil and also as a cold remedy from chemists.

Glycerine

This liquid lubricates and softens stains. It should be diluted with an equal measure of warm water.

Hydrogen peroxide

Use "10" or "20" volume strength—this will be written on the bottle's label. Dilute 1 part hydrogen peroxide to 4 parts water.

Going Green

Lemon juice, white vinegar, glycerine, eucalyptus oil, and baking soda are all natural store cupboard basics that between them work on many stains but won't harm the environment.

SPRING CLEANING
IS "SING" CLEANING
leaning
for safe smooth cleaning
"for every job from A to Z!"

Mythbuster!

Who hasn't poured salt over spilled red wine? All wrong, it seems. Research shows that salt—or another favorite remedy, white wine—is just a messy waste of time. The best solution is a mix of liquid soap and hydrogen peroxide—the chemical used to bleach hair. And if the cloth was originally white, a weak solution of household bleach works best. White wine, which is said to wash away the stain, in fact does nothing, while that pinch of salt to draw out the spilt liquid simply helps to set the stain!

Lemon juice
A mild, natural alternative to bleach, lemon juice cuts through grease and removes perspiration and other stains.

Rubbing alcohol (surgical spirit)
This is useful for removing stains caused by glue, pen ink, and crayons.

White vinegar
Use this on nongreasy, water-based stains, but wash it out thoroughly before drying. Use 1 part vinegar to 5 parts water.

Washing soda (sodium carbonate)
This cleans clothes, softens water, cuts through grease, disinfects, and increases the cleaning power of soap. A strong solution should shift tea, coffee, blood, and ink stains.

You'll also need plenty of absorbent materials such as paper towels, clean white cotton rags or cloths, cotton balls or swabs, and a soft brush and sponge.

Those Tricky Stains

These methods outwit even some of the most difficult stains to shift.

Adhesives

For household and contact glue dab with acetone (not on acetate) then rinse the stain with warm water. PVA or fish or animal glue should be washed off with cold water. Latex should be washed with warm, soapy water and then rinsed.

Ballpoint-pen ink

Dab the ink stain gently with a cloth or cotton ball dipped in a solution of hydrogen peroxide or methyl alcohol. Rinse or give it a warm wash if possible.

Blood

Sponge fresh stains with cold water, blot dry, then shampoo if necessary. On fabric sponge with cold saltwater then machine-wash immediately with biological detergent. Dried stains are hard to remove and may need professional cleaning, but try soaking them with washing soda or a pre-wash product. On furnishings (including mattresses) sponge fresh stains with cold water. Stubborn stains can be soaked in hydrogen peroxide solution ("20" volume strength: 1 part to 4 parts water) plus a few drops of ammonia.

Chewing gum

If the item is small enough, put it into the freezer until the gum sets completely hard and brittle, then gently chip it off. For larger items apply an ice cube, until the gum becomes

Bill is just a normal lad
sometimes good and sometimes bad
but everywhere he goes they find
he leaves a mark or stain behind

hard. Any remaining spots can be cleaned off with a white vinegar solution.

Crayon

Dab with white spirit to remove the greasy element. Soak for about an hour in a glycerine solution (1 part to 2 parts water), then wash in detergent in the usual way.

Felt-tip pen

Dab the stain lightly with either methyl alcohol or grease solvent. (A cotton ball is ideal for this purpose.) Wash as usual.

Mildew

Washable items such as nylon shower curtains can be machine-washed in biological detergent. White items not made of nylon can be cleaned with a solution of hydrogen peroxide ("20" volume strength: 1 part to 4 parts cold water) or a paste made of borax and vinegar.

Paint—emulsion

Scrape or sponge off as much as possible immediately while the paint is still wet. Wash clothes at once in biological detergent. Sponge upholstery with warm, soapy water, rinse, and then blot dry with paper towel.

Paint—oil based

Oil, or solvent-based, paint is unlikely to come out completely, and the treatment may remove color from fabric. Scrape off the excess, dab with mineral spirit, and then wash as usual in detergent. For upholster, sponge with warm, soapy water, rinse, and then blot dry with paper towel.

Perspiration

Fresh stains can be treated with a solution of ammonia (1 part to 3 parts water), then rinsed. Alternatively, dab with lemon juice or white vinegar solution—1 tablespoon (15ml) vinegar to half a of pint (250ml) water—and leave for 5 minutes. Then soak in a biological detergent and wash in the normal manner. These stains can be difficult to remove completely. For nonwashable items dab gently with the vinegar solution to clear the stain and freshen up the area.

Tar

On carpet or furnishings dab with eucalyptus oil and then sponge with warm, soapy water or wash as usual. You can also try rubbing in peanut butter and then washing as normal.

Urine

Sponge old stains with ammonia solution—1 tablespoon (15ml) to 1 pint (500ml) of cold water—then apply shampoo or wash in biological detergent. You can also try sponging first with a vinegar solution: 1 tablespoon (15ml) to 1 pint (500ml) of cold water).

Wax

Scrape off as much of the surface wax as possible. Place kitchen paper or brown paper over the residue and iron off using a warm iron, being careful not to let the iron touch the carpet or fabric as it may scorch it. Move the paper around so that clean sections can absorb the wax. Any residual color can be removed by dabbing with colorless methyl alcohol before washing. On hard surfaces lift as much as possible with a plastic spatula or fingernail, then clean or polish as normal.

Wine

If the stain has dried, soften with glycerine (1 part to 2 parts water) before washing. Rinse in warm water, then sponge with borax solution: 1 tablespoon (15ml) to 1 pint (500ml) of water) if necessary. Wash in the usual manner.

Chocolate

Soak your stain with club soda and then wash. Alternatively, mix 1 teaspoon (5ml) of a neutral detergent (a mild detergent containing no alkalis or bleaches) with 1 cup (240ml) of lukewarm water and blot. Then mix 1 tablespoon of household ammonia with half cup of water and blot again. Next repeat step one before sponging with clean water. Finish by blotting.

Coffee

Follow the instructions for "Chocolate" above, but instead of using a solution of household ammonia at the second stage, use one-third of a cup of white household vinegar with two-thirds cup of water. To remove coffee from walls and work surfaces, make a paste of baking soda and water. Apply to the mark, leave for 15 minutes, and wipe away.

Ink

Put some cream of tartar on the stain with a few drops of water from an ice cube dripped over the top. Rub into the stain then brush off the powder with a clean brush. Sponge the stain with warm water. If it doesn't work the first time, repeat the process (immediately).

Lipstick

Rub vegetable oil into the stain and allow it to soak for 15 minutes. Blot any excess oil with a paper towel. Next sponge in a solution of 50% ammonia with water (unless the fabric is silk or wool), rinse thoroughly with cool water, and wring out.

Sponge the remaining stain liberally with surgical spirit. Apply laundry pre-treatment detergent and wash washables in hot water.

Lipstick contains a lot of dye in even a tiny particle so you might prefer to take the item to a professional—perhaps a local dry-cleaner —who can deal with the problem expertly.

Your own cleaner in a bottle

Did you know that even without the powerful stain removers that you can buy in the stores you probably have the ingredients for effective stain removal in your home already? The remedies that our parents and grandparents used are just as relevant today and you can easily look up these alternative, low–chemical cleaning methods on the inter–net or in books. It's as if your mom or grandma are there to give you a helping hand!

chapter 4

Caring for Special Things

Looking after Antiques

Look after antique furniture and it will last for years and increase in value. Handle it carefully, display it in the right conditions, and if necessary be willing to call in the experts—it's best to leave restoration to a professional. Botched amateur repairs will devalue an item and may not be easily reversible. For instance, if you use the wrong type of glue it can result in having to pay for a pricey professional repair later. When a breakage occurs carefully collect each broken piece, no matter how tiny, wrap them in acid-free tissue paper, and place them in a box to prevent further damage or loss.

Keep your antiques safe

If you have valuables you should invest in some good home security measures and ensure that they can be identified if they are stolen.

Take close-up, individual color photos of all your valuable items, against a plain background, with something like a ruler or coin alongside to indicate its real size. Take extra photos of any distinguishing marks. Make a detailed inventory of your valuables and keep it in a secure place with the photos. Keep a second copy of the inventory and photos elsewhere, perhaps in a bank or with a lawyer.

Mark precious items with your name and zip code using a security marker pen on any part that is not visible or else attach electronic security tabs to them.

Insurance companies usually require antiques to be valued by a reputable dealer or valuer. Keep the valuation documents in a safe place and have them updated from time to time because values can fluctuate.

The Household Genie's Tip

Take close-up photos of valuable items against a white background with a size indicator such as a ruler or coin next to it as a record in case of theft. Keep one copy at home and another in a safe place such as a bank or lawyer's office, or even with a friend.

Caring for Antique Furniture

Handle antique furniture with respect—don't tilt back on chairs, open drawers using just one of two handles, or drag fine furniture around. Lift tables from the lowest part of the main frame rather than lifting from the top surface. Lift chairs from beneath the seat. Old furniture that has a surface patina, acquired over the years and possibly even with marks, combines character with value, and should be looked after.

Cleaning and polishing

Waxing every few months with a good-quality polish based on beeswax protects the wood and brings out the color and grain. Put a small amount of polish on a soft cloth and rub gently to burnish, then polish with a clean duster. Applying wax at night, leaving it, then polishing the next day nourishes the wood. Dust often with a clean, dry, soft duster.

If you need to clean a piece of furniture, use a soft, damp cloth or chamois leather well wrung out. A weak solution of vinegar and water can be used to clean more thoroughly

but use this only on polished, undamaged wood. After cleaning wipe again with a clean cloth rinsed in clean water then dry at once with absorbent paper or a soft dry cloth.

Deal quickly with spills and wet rings left by glasses, but allow wet areas to dry thoroughly before applying wax. If you apply wax while the wood is still damp, more is absorbed on the damp part than the surrounding area, leading to staining.

Brass mounts and handles should not be polished with cleaners intended for metal because they can harm the wood around them. A light rub while dusting should be enough to keep them bright.

Vacuum upholstery regularly to guard against a build-up of dust and pests.

Light, heat, and humidity

Sunlight and humidity as well as central heating and pollutants in the air can affect organic materials such as wood, fabric, and leather. So it pays to give some thought to the environment in which antiques are kept.

Do not keep fine furniture in strong sunlight, which will fade its color. Keep out rays with roller blinds, or draw the curtains when a room is not in use.

Dealing with pests

If your furniture has woodworm, you'll soon know about it. Wood beetles lay their eggs in tiny crevices in wood; the eggs hatch into larvae—woodworm—which eat into the wood, leaving small tunnels. Eventually they become beetles and fly away, usually during the summer months, which is when you can most easily check for new holes and deposits of dust, which indicate active infestation. Woodworm spreads, so deal with the problem as soon as possible.

You can usually put a stop to woodworm with special fluid to kill the eggs, but use it only on the unfinished surfaces of the wood because solvent in the fluid will damage surfaces with any kind of finish. Look for low-odor products, which are less toxic but just as effective as solvent-based ones. After treatment the wormholes can be disguised with soft wax. Other treatments are available from specialists, including a warm-air treatment that involves no chemicals or toxins.

Restoration

If a piece of antique furniture needs proper restoration, do consult a professional restorer. Attempting to do it on your own may well devalue it. If you decide to carry out minor

Fluctuations in temperature and humidity can damage furniture, and central heating dries the air—humidifiers can help here. Just placing a bowl of water in a room can help. Damp rooms can also cause problems, so use a dehumidifier if necessary. The ideal humidity level is around 50 to 55 percent—check regularly with humidity indicator cards, strips, or even a garden hygrometer. Keep room temperatures as constant as possible—install a thermostat if necessary—and air rooms well.

Going Green
If you don't like using chemical insecticides but you have a woodworm problem, try rubbing garlic into the wood. Apparently the worms don't like the taste.

"But darling, wouldn't it be awfully hard work to keep it looking good?"

repairs, use water-soluble wood glue. Small chips of wood, veneer, etc., can be held in place with low-tack masking tape while the glue is setting or before to professional restoration. Drawers and doors that stick can be eased by rubbing candle wax on the surface. Dry, cracked leather on desktops can be revitalized with a lanolin and beeswax cream, but do check a small area first in case it stains. You can also use clear, neutral shoe cream or leather cream.

Looking after Rare Books

If you have spent a lot of money on editions of rare books that you love, you'll want them to last for as long as possible.

Here are a few things that you can do to make your valuable book collection look good for as long as you have it.

When you first buy your books, put them in the fridge to kill any bugs that might be in them. From thereon keep your books in a cool dry place. Overheating causes books to dry out and shrink, and the binding will crack and break. However, although you need to keep your precious books in a cool place, be aware that keeping them in a basement won't be good for them either if the basement is damp. Damp causes all types of trouble, including staining, mold, and insects.

Try to keep your books stored away from sunlight wherever possible. Sunlight will fade a dust jacket (on rare books you want to keep your dust jacket in good condition, as well as the cover) and bleach color from both cloth covers and the book's pages.

Dust your books regularly. To remove large amounts of dust vaccum the bok on a low setting, holding it firmly shut to prevent dust from falling between the pages. For lighter dust coverings you should use one of the new types of cloth that hold dust electro-magnetically. Do not use a regular duster because it will only redistribute dust. Although there are specialist book-cover cleaners available, an electromagnetic cloth, which is free of chemicals that might be harmful over several years is arguably better.

Clean your bookshelves regularly, using an electromagnetic duster. For heavier stains on a bookshelf use detergent and water only and avoid chemical cleaners that might harm the covers. Be sure that the shelves are completely dry before you replace the books.

Antique Silver and Metalwork

Antiques made from metal should be treated as gently as those made from materials such as glass or porcelain. Metal may seem hard but in fact the most sought-after metals tend to be quite soft, so always use the softest of cloths and wear cotton gloves to avoid damaging the surface.

Silver

Silver should not be handled and cleaned more than necessary. Dust regularly with a soft cloth, using a soft brush for crevices, or wash in warm, soapy water—not a dishwasher—rinsing well and drying with kitchen paper. Tarnish is harmless but looks unsightly, so keep it to a minimum by storing silver wrapped in acid-free tissue paper, cotton that has not been dyed, or linen, and keep it in airtight conditions when not on display.

Tarnishing can be caused by humidity, sulfurous foods such as egg yolks or Brussels sprouts, or grubby fingers. Always wear cotton gloves while cleaning or dusting silver. Remove tarnishing with non-abrasive, effective products such as impregnated cloths, silver foam, or polish. Don't reuse silver dip too many times because the particles of silver that collect in the jar can then leave a patchy deposit on other pieces being cleaned.

Rinse after cleaning in clean water and dry with paper towel or a clean tea towel. Brush out dried polish from crevices with a dry, soft brush. Never use steel wool or an abrasive cloth to remove stains because they will scratch the surface. A tiny amount of metal will be removed at each cleaning, especially with silver-plate ware, which can eventually lose its finish completely, so polish as seldom as possible.

Silver turns green if it comes into contact with salt, so salt cellars should always be gilt- or glass-lined and the salt should be removed from them after use.

Another safe method of cleaning silver or plated items is with a chemical dip. Line a plastic bowl with aluminum foil and place the silver on it. Wearing rubber gloves, dissolve half a cup of washing soda in 2 pints of very

Mythbuster!

Silver does not require the rigorous polishing you might think. In fact, as a soft metal, it should be handled as infrequently and as gently as possible.

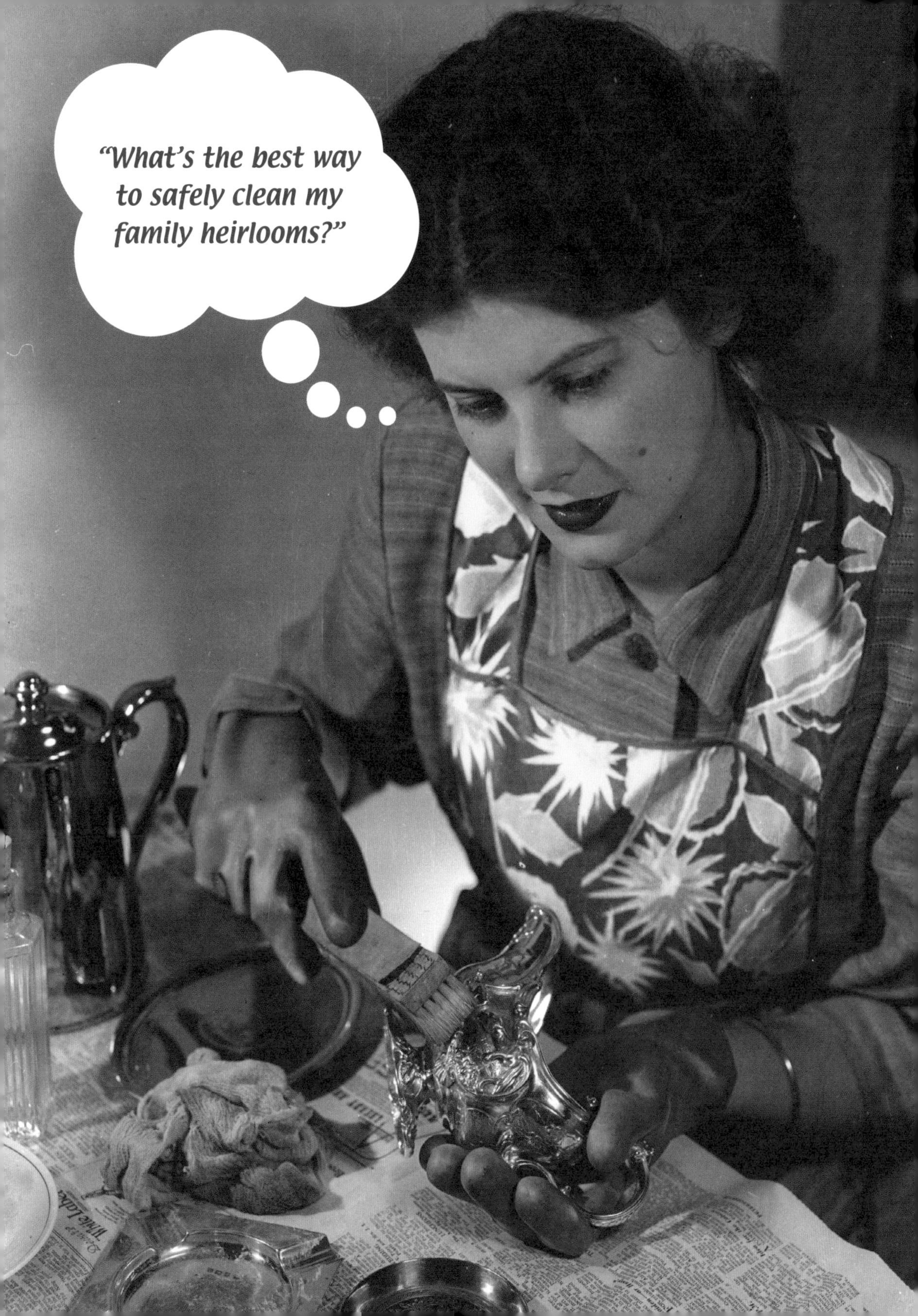
"What's the best way to safely clean my family heirlooms?"

hot water and pour it over. The solution will bubble as the corrosion is transferred chemically from the silver to the aluminum. Wait a couple of minutes, then remove the silver pieces using wooden tongs or a wooden spoon and rinse under hot water, dry, and polish it immediately. This dip can also be used for copper and brass, but don't clean different metals in the same dip.

Gold

A gold object may be solid or plated, silver gilt, or ormolu, so establish which before cleaning it. Gold is very soft and scratches easily; a thin layer on silver can easily rub off. It should be handled with care but it does not tarnish unless it has a high silver content (for instance, in the case of some 9-carat gold). Stick to light dusting or gentle washing in warm, soapy water.

Pewter

Pewter is also easily scratched and dented. Its high lead content will lead to corrosion if it comes into contact with anything acid such as oak, so it is best to keep pewter pieces away from oak furniture. A heavily stained or very dull surface can be successfully treated by gently wiping it with a cloth impregnated with linseed oil and talcum powder. This should then be removed with cotton wool moistened with methyl alcohol, washed, rinsed, and dried. It's entirely up to you whether your pewter is kept highly polished to a silvery finish, allowed to develop a dark, matte surface, or matured to a soft gleam by regular light buffing with a dry soft cloth.

Copper and brass

Copper and brass naturally develop a soft patina, which is a plus point on antique items and should not be cleaned off with metal polishes. Instead, buff regularly with a soft cloth or chamois leather to keep the metals clean, but bear in mind that both metals scratch easily. Heavy staining can be removed with copper or brass cleaners or impregnated wadding, while a light tarnish can be rubbed off with a specialist silver cloth. A good alternative to brand cleaners is a mix 1 level tablespoon (25g) of salt with 1 tablespoon (15 ml) of vinegar in half a pint (250 ml) of hot water and then, using extremely fine steel wool, wipe brass with the solution without rubbing hard. For copper use a rough cloth rather than wire wool. Wash in hot, soapy water, rinse, dry, and then apply polish.

Jewelry

Cleaning jewelry should be approached gently, starting with simple brushing with a soft, clean, small paintbrush. Check that settings are secure. Some pieces are set with glue and these should not be cleaned with any liquid since it might loosen the setting. Hard stones such as diamonds, rubies, sapphires, and amethysts can usually be cleaned in warm water and dishwashing liquid, using a small brush, and dried thoroughly with a lint-free cloth. Soft stones such as opals, turquoise, and pearls should only be polished with a soft cloth. Make sure that you do your cleaning where any pieces that do come loose can be recovered, such as over a plastic bowl lined with an old towel.

Paintings, Drawings, and Photos

Oil paintings, ink drawings, and even good pencil sketches need care and attention to maintain their condition and value.

Paintings and drawings

■ Hanging

It really pays to hang pictures securely. Strong nylon cord is ideal; brass or copper picture wire is fine, too, as long as you check the metal for corrosion occasionally. Eye hooks should be screwed into the frame, but for smaller pictures hooks can be fixed to the backboard if you attach a barrier to prevent contact with the work. The strength of the hook and its fixing into the wall should be sturdy enough to bear the weight of the picture. It's best to use two hooks for extra strength and to stop the picture from moving.

Avoid hanging pictures over a fireplace or radiator, unless there is a mantelpiece or radiator shelf, because heat and smoke could harm the picture. Avoid direct sunlight, too, since it can cause fading. Don't hang pictures on damp walls. To help air circulate and to protect from dampness, especially if hung on an outside wall, allow a picture to lean away slightly from the wall at the top. You can also add a little padding by gluing a small pad made from, for example, a thin slice of a cork from a wine bottle, to the bottom corners of the back of the frame. Damp can leave brown tidemarks or cause paper to ripple when it dries out, while very dry conditions, often caused by central heating, can make paper dehydrate and crack, so use a dehumidifier or humidifier if necessary.

■ Framing and mounting

Because a coat of varnish already protects them, traditionally oil paintings are framed without glass. But works on paper— watercolors, drawings, and prints—should be glazed. Perspex is lighter and less fragile than glass, but scratches easily and attracts dust. Special UV filter glass is expensive but worth it for valuable pictures because it can filter out up to 95 percent of harmful UV rays.

Works on paper should be set behind an acid-free card window mount to separate the glass from the artwork, preventing rubbing and providing circulation of air to deter mold.

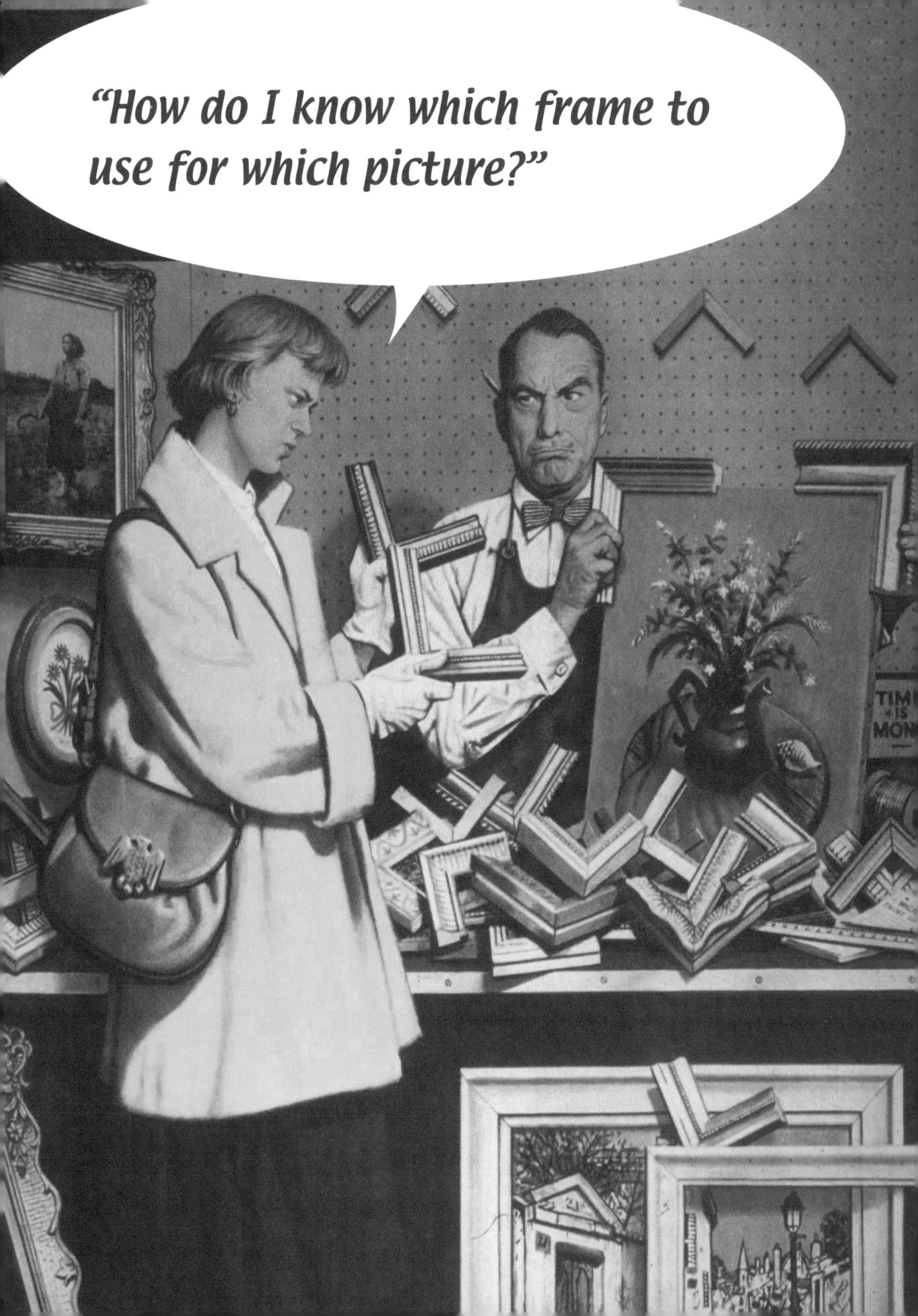
"How do I know which frame to use for which picture?"

■ **Storage**

Oil paintings and other valuable pictures on paper that are not displayed must be stored somewhere clean, dry, dark, and where the temperature is cool and fairly constant. Keep paintings upright and off the floor on blocks, with acid-free board between each one. Stack the largest and heaviest at the back and remove any picture hooks so that they don't damage the next frame or canvas. Cover the stack with a clean dustsheet (do not use plastic because it can cause mold). Unframed works on paper, such as maps or prints, are best kept flat in acid-free boxes or folders with acid-free tissue paper between each work.

■ **Cleaning**

Apart from dusting frames and the glass protecting works on paper, picture cleaning should be done only by a skilled professional. Never clean gilded frames with a damp cloth or sponge as this will eventually remove the gold leaf. Inspect your pictures regularly for signs of decay such as flaking oil paint, dirty varnish, and surface mold, which should be dealt with professionally.

Looking after photographs

Photos—both old and new—are precious to all of us and we want to be able to store our photographic memories for ever. However, the nature of photography is such that there is no guarantee that your photos will remain unchanged forever. You can't clean photos, but how you store them will make a great difference to their longevity.

Store your photos somewhere neither too dry nor damp, with a consistent temperature

of around 67°F (19°C) and handle them touching only the edges of the paper or wearing cotton gloves. Do not use paper clips to hold photos because they will scratch the surfaces and avoid rubber bands that will give off corrosive sulfer. If you want to caption your photographs, write on the back using an acid-free photo-marking pen or soft lead pencil avoiding acid ink that will, over time, stain and ruin your photos.

Invest in good-quality photo albums that are specifically made for storing photos and don't keep your precious memories in plastic bags. Finally, don't store your prints with your negatives—keeping them separate means that if something happens to one, you still have the other as back-up.

Porcelain and Pottery

Ceramic is the generic term for all items made from clay and fired in a kiln, and which may end up as porcelain, pottery, or stoneware. The word "china" is not used for antiques except for bone china, which is a hard-paste porcelain mixed with animal-bone ash to make it whiter.

Handling and display

Always pick up an item by the body, supporting it from underneath rather than by a handle, spout, or head. Valuable or delicate pieces are best displayed in a cabinet in which the shelves should be stable to avoid vibrations. Do not use adhesive tape to hold on lids or other loose parts as it can damage the glaze and remove gilding or decoration. Instead, use low-tack sticky putty. If you like displaying cut flowers or plants in antique pottery or porcelain, place a separate container in the piece with a protective pad between the two. Damaged plates should not be hung on a wall. When hanging plates or displaying them on shelves use acrylic or plastic-coated fittings or stands that can be adjusted to fit.

Cleaning

Before washing remove dirt and dust from any decorative pieces using a soft, dry brush. Glazed ceramics that have not been restored can safely be washed in warm water with a little dishwashing liquid, but don't use abrasive cleaners on them or place in a dishwasher. Protect items by laying a towel or sponge at the bottom of the bowl, which should ideally be plastic. Rinse well and leave to dry on a clean towel. You can use a warm hairdryer on a low setting for drying intricate items, or leave them in the airing cupboard overnight to dry.

Unglazed pieces may be porous so they should not be left to soak in water. Instead, clean them with a soft cloth or cotton balls soaked in soapy water. Objects with ormolu or other metal fittings, or those mended with iron rivets, should also not be soaked in water. Some stains on porcelain (but not on pieces with gilt or luster decoration) can be removed by applying cotton balls soaked in a solution of "20" volume hydrogen peroxide and a few drops of ammonia. The cotton balls should be left in position for an hour or two but not allowed to dry out. Don't use household bleach because although this appears to give a good result for a while, it will eventually lead to an unpleasant yellowing of the item.

Glass

Glass should be stored in dry, ventilated conditions because damp can cause white, cloudy stains. A damp glass can be permanently stained in a few hours by strong sunlight. Decanters should not be stored with their stoppers in place in case there is remaining damp inside.

Cleaning

Glass that is old, valuable, or delicate should never be washed in a dishwasher. It must always be washed by hand, ideally, in a plastic bowl of tepid water and washing detergent, lined with a thick towel for protection. Before you begin to wash, to avoid scratching the glass, remove all rings and watches.

To dry the inside of decanters or slim-necked vases, place them upside down in an airing cupboard for a day. You can also roll up some paper tissues (paper towels might scratch delicate glass), and push the roll gently into a decanter until it touches the bottom, then remove it the following day.

Use a very soft brush, for example a traditional shaving or makeup brush, to work gently into crevices. Clean the inside of a decanter by simply swishing around a handful of rice grains mixed with some detergent and warm water.

Hard water left in glass can leave calcium deposits, and alcohol will often leave dark stains; both can be treated with citric acid, white vinegar, or a mixture of 1 tablespoon of salt (25g) to one-quarter of a pint (125 ml) of vinegar. Leave in the glass or decanter for 24 hours, shaking occasionally, then rinse, and dry thoroughly. Do not use stronger acids, since they may etch into old glass. Very old glass or glass that has a fine network of cracks should not be washed, and should be handled as little as possible.

If you break a valued glassware item, do not attempt to glue it back together yourself—take it to a repair specialist instead who can give it the expert care and attention it needs.

Textiles

Antique textiles need careful handling because they can be easily damaged. Textiles can become stained from general dirt, rust, chemicals, food, mold, insect droppings, or the decomposition of the fibers so it's vital that you know good, effective ways of keeping your textiles at their best.

Vacuuming can cause damage to fibers, but if the material is fairly resilient you can cover it with a microfilament net and vacuum on a very low power setting. Stop immediately if you see fibers rather than dirt coming off. Reasonably robust pillowcases, christening gowns, lace items, etc., can be washed by hand using nonbiological detergent, rinsed in warm water and dried flat. Delicate pieces can be layed flat on a padded board covered with white cotton fabric, gently sponged with mild detergent, and rinsed with cold water. If an item needs further cleaning or you're not sure what the material can stand up to, talk to a textile conservator, and certainly don't be tempted to use boiling water or chemicals, even soda crystals, with old textiles.

Handling and storage

To be on the safe side, wear clean, white cotton gloves and look closely at a textile before moving it. It may be more fragile than it seems. If a piece of costume is on a hanger, use the hanger to hold it. If you are moving a small, flat textile, you can carry it safely by sliding a piece of clean cardboard underneath it. Pieces of costume should be cradled in a white sheet and carried with both hands.

Textiles should be stored carefully in large tubes, acid-free boxes, or on a hanger. If textiles, especially costume, have to be stored on hangers, use a sturdy hanger that follows the shoulder shape of the garment. Wrap the hanger with flame-retardant polyester padding to make it softer.

Don't use plastic to cover textiles because this can attract dust through static electricity, and the plastic can develop condensation, which encourages mold. Instead, use clean, white cotton or a blend of polyester and cotton to cover your textiles. Try to give them enough hanging space so they are not crushed against other items.

It is best to store large, flat textiles face upward carefully wrapped around a large tube, ideally an acid-free type that will not discolor the fibers. If you can't find one, use a cardboard roll or even a length of plastic piping, so long as it's at least as wide as a coffee mug and clean inside with no ragged ends. Cover it with four or five layers of acid-free tissue paper and carefully roll the piece, keeping it smooth.

Acid-free boxes are also good, especially for large or bulky items; ideally they should be large enough to avoid folding the textiles. Line the box with acid-free tissue paper with enough slack over the edges to fold over the final layers. If you have to fold textiles, roll up tissue paper and place it inside the fold.

chapter 5

Good Housekeeping

Sewing Magic

You don't need to be an expert needlewoman to carry out basic sewing repairs and maintenance, and looking after your clothes will save you money in the long run. Your basic workbox should contain several needles of different sizes, iron-on hems, spools of various colors of thread, buttons, pins, a tape measure, safety pins, and scissors.

Sewing machines

A few tips should keep your sewing machine in tip-top condition.

Sharpening needles: stitch through a piece of fine sandpaper to sharpen your sewing-machine needles.

Steadying machines: stop your sewing machine from sliding around by standing it on a foam-backed carpet tile or a piece of bubble wrap. Stick some foam rubber to the underside of the machine's foot control.

Removing lint: a small paint brush or cosmetic brush can be used to remove lint from around the bobbin.

Sewing tips to save time

■ Keep clear thread in your sewing kit for speedy, invisible mending.

■ Make a rust-free pin cushion from a fabric bag filled with dry, used coffee grounds, or use a bar of soap.

■ Store spare buttons on a safety pin or length of wool, or string, for safekeeping.

■ To thread cord or elastic through a hem, pin one end to a large safety pin and feed it through, scrunching and sliding the fabric along the pin as you go.

■ A stuck zipper can be loosened by rubbing a little liquid soap onto the teeth.

■ Place a hairpin under a button when sewing it onto a garment to allow space for the buttonhole to fit over it.

■ When removing buttons slide a comb under it to lift the button before cutting it off.

■ Sew four-hole buttons two holes at a time, finishing off the thread in between so the buttons will not fall off if they become loose.

■ Tears in bed linen or clothes can be invisibly mended by pulling the edges together and patching the reverse of the material with an iron-on adhesive patch.

The Household Genie's Tip

When sewing buttons onto children's clothes, use dental floss or elastic thread for extra strength.

■ When a hem drops and cannot be mended immediately, use a piece of adhesive tape for a quick fix. A speedy but short-term alternative to sewing a hem is iron-on invisible mending tape.

■ Stop runs in stockings and panty hose (tights) by dabbing on a little clear nail polish at the top and bottom of the run.

■ If you find it hard to coax a piece of thread through the eye of a needle, wipe a little soap or petroleum jelly on the thread to keep it rigid and stop the ends from splitting.

■ A pocket with a hole can be mended by cutting away any frayed material and then creating a new seam higher up.

■ To mend a split seam simply turn the garment inside out and sew the seam again using a simple running stitch (or better still, using a sewing machine if you can).

■ If you're hemming curtains, hang the curtains for a few days before doing any cutting or sewing because the material will stretch slightly as it hangs.

■ To avoid thread becoming twisted or tangled, use no more than 20in (50cm) of thread, extending from the needle.

■ Choose the right needle and thread for each job. Use double thread where you might need extra strength, such as buttonholes.

Knitting

■ If you're mending a knitted garment, place the torn part over the back of a wide hairbrush so it doesn't stretch.

■ Keep a couple of pipe cleaners handy if you're a knitter to keep hold of dropped stitches until you can pick them up.

■ When knitting with more than one color, you can separate the yarn, by putting the balls in a net plastic shopping bag and pulling each one through a different hole.

Hems

Ask the person who is going to wear the garment to put it on to make accurate alterations or use a tape measure or existing hemlines as a guide. If the existing hem is straight, cut the fabric to about 2in (5cm) below the length you want it to be. Turn the garment inside out, turn up the raw edge by about ¾in (2cm) pinning it all around as you go, and press it with an iron. Remove the pins and turn up the remaining 1¼in (3cm) then pin and press again. Make large stitches on the inside of the garment, catching a single strand of fiber each time on the outside of the garment. Lay trousers flat on a table to check that both hems are even.

The Best for your Pets

Before you buy a pet ask a vet (or consult a book) about its diet and care needs so you are fully informed before you commit yourself. You pet will need regular feeding with a varied diet, somewhere to exercise, and a ready supply of clean drinking water. If you feel unsure, see if you can borrow a similar pet from someone else for a couple of weeks. Or arrange to walk a neighbor's dog—you may be surprised by how much care and attention they need. Don't buy a pet just because your children insist they want one—be realistic about who will end up with most of the responsibility for its wellbeing!

Getting rid of pet odors

■ Place a small dish of vinegar in the room where a dog sleeps, or near a cat-litter tray, to absorb odors. To deodorize cat litter, add 1 part of laundry borax to 6 parts of cat litter, or 8oz (225g) of bicarbonate of soda to a tray of litter.

Parasites

■ Use a flea collar or powder, or rub citrus oil into your pet's fur to discourage fleas and ticks. Pennyroyal oil or tea tree oil under a collar is another method. You can make a herbal flea collar from a roll of fabric stuffed with tansy and catnip.

■ To kill lice (eggs or nits) wash your pet once every two weeks in a weak solution of white vinegar and water.

Cleaning pets

■ When bathing dogs put an old tea strainer in the drain hole to catch hairs. Add vinegar or lemon juice to the rinse water to eliminate any soap smell.

■ Give a dry bath by rubbing bicarbonate of soda into your dog's coat, then brushing it out.

Going Green

Pets dislike the smell and taste of oil of cloves, so wipe some on furniture legs to stop a new puppy from chewing them or kittens using it as a scratching post.

Going Green: a Healthier Household

These days we're bombarded with all kinds of chemicals and it's no wonder that many people are seriously concerned about what they may be doing to our health—and our children's—in the long term. Increasing affluence also means that we're constantly consuming, which has all kinds of repercussions on our environment. It's our responsibility to look after the planet, and even small measures will us to help play our part.

Painting and renovating: solvent-based household paints give off dangerous fumes. Where possible choose water-based alternatives, which contain fewer volatile organic compounds (VOCs).

Toys: toys made from PVC plastic can contain softeners called phthalates, which are suspected hormone disrupters, so try to buy PVC-free toys. In Europe new teething toys must be free from phthalates.

Food: organic food is produced without using artificial chemical pesticides, but buy from a reputable supplier and look for accreditation labels.

Bottles and beakers: plastic baby bottles, beakers, and tableware made from polycarbonate can leak potentially risky chemicals when worn or scratched so replace at the first sign of damage.

Scents: some perfumes and scented products, such as air fresheners, contain suspect chemicals like artificial musk. It's often difficult to tell from the ingredients list what these products contain, so it makes sense to cut down on your use of them. Open a window or explore gentler, natural and homemade alternatives instead. (See pages 30–32 for suggestions.)

Household products: choose environmentally friendly products where possible to reduce the amount of chemicals entering the environment, and explore natural alternatives. (See Cleaning and Revitalizing on pages 29–57.)

Why recycle?

It has been estimated that each household produces about one tonne of garbage annually, an amount that is continuing to grow thanks to more sophisticated packaging, more fast food, increased buying of consumer goods, and more leisure time. But you could reduce your

■ Recycling means that less waste goes to landfill sites or incinerators so there is less waste disposal impact on the environment.

Ways to recycle

■ Find out about local facilities for recycling newspapers, glass, cans, etc.
■ Build a compost heap for your organic kitchen and garden refuse.
■ Avoid buying excessively packaged goods.
■ Use your own shopping bags or boxes.
■ Buy loose food rather than pre-packaged.
■ Reuse plastic shopping bags.
■ Reuse paper for scrap.
■ Use refillable containers.
■ Reuse envelopes.
■ Give your unwanted clothes and furniture to charity.
■ Cancel the delivery of unwanted free newspapers and find out the best way to stop junk mail coming through your door.
■ Be creative with old things. For instance, turn worn tablecloths into napkins, sheets into children's nightwear or pillowcases, girls' dresses into patchwork quilts, and plastic raincoats into protective covers for schoolbooks and cookbooks.

household's waste by more than 50 percent. Recycling is becoming easier, with an increasing number of local authorities taking steps to help consumers play their part. How each household can help varies from area to area and even country to country, but the basics include taking bottles, cardboard, newspapers, cans, clothes, appliances, and car batteries to appropriate collection points. Organic matter can be composted. We should all be recycling unused items and leftovers for these reasons:

■ Recycling cuts down demand for raw materials and thus, destruction of resources.
■ It reduces the waste and damage to the habitat that results when raw materials are farmed or extracted.
■ It saves energy in the production process and reduces emissions into air and water.

Saving energy

We've all heard about "global warming," but how does it happen? Power stations burn fossil fuels to generate energy, and pump out damaging greenhouse gases into the atmosphere. These waste gases heat up the earth like a greenhouse—hence the warming. Global warming refers to the projected change in climate that has already started and is

expected to worsen. Radiation from the sun is usually absorbed by the earth and then re-emitted from its surface. The escape of the radiation is being prevented by various gases in the air—such as carbon dioxide, methane, and chlorofluorocarbons—resulting in a rise in the earth's temperature This rise, melting ice caps and raising sea levels, causes climate change. By reducing energy wastage in your home you will cut down the amount of fuel that you use and ultimately, this will help to slow down global warming because you're producing fewer of the gases that cause it. The following simple measures will help you to achieve this and to reduce your fuel bills at the same time.

Simple tips

First of all, eliminate drafts and wasted heat. Use an easy-to-fix brush or PVC seal on your exterior doors and fill gaps in floorboards and skirting with newspaper, beading, or sealant. Make sure your windows are draftproof. A low cost, short-term alternative to double glazing is to tape polythene across window frames. Remember, however, that ventilation is also important, especially if you have open fireplaces, gas-fueled heaters, or a boiler with a flue. If you have a chimney, get it swept regularly, and check your airbricks for any blockages. Practice some of these energy-saving measures, too:

Heating: Turn your thermostat down by 1° and cut your heating bills by up to 10 percent.

Hot water: Check that it's not too hot. For most people setting the thermostat at 125°F (60°C) is fine for bathing and washing.

Plugs: always put the plug in the drain hole to stop precious hot water from draining away.

Curtains: close your curtains as soon as it gets dark to stop heat from escaping through the windows.

Lights: turn them off when you leave a room.

Fridges: always close the door quickly to stop cold air from escaping and don't put hot or warm food straight into the fridge. If your fridge is not frost-free, defrost it regularly to keep it running efficiently. If you must site your fridge next to an oven or boiler, leave a good gap between them. If you suspect the seal is not working properly, insert a piece of paper and close the fridge door around it. If you can pull it out easily the seal is loose or worn and may need replacing.

Washing machines and tumble dryers: always wash a full load, or use a half-load or economy program. Use the lowest temperature washing program possible. Your clothes will still come out clean because modern washing powders are more effective than ever. Very wet clothes should be wrung out or spin-dried before going into a tumble dryer.

Dishwashers: try the low-temperature program, and ensure you wash a full load.

Pots and pans: choose the right size of pan for the food and the stove and keep lids on when cooking. Use only as much water as you need (this applies to kettles, too).

Faucets: a dripping hot-water faucet can waste enough water to fill a bath in just a day, so check for drips.

Showers: an ordinary shower uses less than half of the water needed for a bath.

Light bulbs: if there's a light that's on for four

hours or more a day, replace it with an energy-saving bulb. These use around a quarter of the electricity and last up to 12 times longer.

Hot-water tank: an insulating jacket for your hot-water cylinder costs very little, but it conserves energy.

Hot water pipes: these can be insulated to stop heat from escaping, especially the pipes between the boiler and hot water cylinder.

Boiler: modern boilers are very efficient and replacing a 15-year-old model could save you more than 20 percent on your fuel bills.

Wall insulation: up to a third of the heat in your home is lost through the walls, so insulating them, if your walls are suitable, is one of the most cost-effective ways to save energy around the home.

Double glazing: your home could be losing up to 20 percent of its heat through single-glazed and poorly insulated window frames. Double glazing can cut these losses by over a half.

Cut your fuel costs

fit double-glazing units

Dealing with Allergies

The majority of people with allergic asthma are sensitive to house-dust mites, or more specifically their droppings, so it makes sense to get rid of them as far as possible if someone in your family is a sufferer. Eczema sufferers can also be affected by dust mites. Try these steps:

- Use a completely enclosing barrier cover for your mattress and wipe it with a damp cloth weekly.
- Wash bedding once a week at 125°F (60°C) or above.
- Keep soft toys to a minimum. Hot wash them every week or two.
- Damp dust all surfaces daily and vacuum all carpeted areas frequently with a powerful cleaner that has a filtered exhaust.
- Use cotton or synthetic blankets rather than wool. They are easier to wash and are less likely to carry allergens.
- There is no conclusive evidence to show that synthetic, "hypo-allergenic" pillows are better than feather ones (unless you're allergic

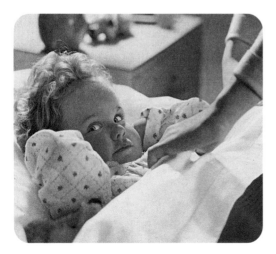

to feathers specifically) but, either way, use a dust mite barrier cover and wipe with a damp cloth weekly.
- Replace carpets with hard flooring such as linoleum, vinyl, rubber, tiles or wood, which can be washed.
- Plain, wooden bed frames are preferable to upholstered beds or headboards, which tend to collect dust.
- Once every two or three months, wash your curtains. Blinds are often a better choice, but make sure you keep them free from dust.

Reduce humidity

House-dust mites thrive in warm and humid environments, so use the following tips to reduce humidity levels in your home:
- Keep rooms well aired.
- Use an extractor fan and/or open windows during and after cooking, when you are doing the washing, and when using the bathroom.
- Keep the kitchen and bathroom doors closed to prevent damp from spreading to other parts of the house.
- Remove any damp and mold in the house quickly and try to avoid condensation by keeping the house well aired.
- If you hang wet clothes indoors, open windows or use a dryer with an outside vent.
- A dehumidifier that reduces indoor humidity may be helpful, but they can be expensive.

Keeping your Houseplants Happy

It makes sense to choose houseplants that like the conditions in your home and your lifestyle. For instance, cacti like warm, sunny rooms, while ferns and ivy are shade lovers. If you tend to overwater, azaleas will be quite happy with this, and bromeliads are tolerant when you forget.

Plants need feeding regularly to encourage them to flower, produce new roots, and maintain healthy leaf growth. And do talk to your plants by all means—you are breathing carbon dioxide on them, which they need in order to survive. You can look out for pests and diseases or signs of stress, too.

As well as looking good, houseplants help increase feelings of relaxation and wellbeing, absorb toxins such as carbon monoxide and VOCs, and help you to breathe more easily. They also release more than 90 percent of the water you give them, helping to humidify the atmosphere.

Top tips for successful plant care

■ Buy plants from a reputable source and inspect them before you buy.

■ Pay attention to the natural habitat of the plant, and its preferred light and heat levels. Try to reproduce the conditions your plant would enjoy in the wild.

■ Most plants prefer to dry out after a thorough watering.

■ Water a plant from below. Stand pots in a dish of water until all the water has been taken up. If you live in a hard-water area, use cool, boiled water.

■ Feed plants regularly to keep them healthy.

■ Plants that like high humidity need regular, preferably daily misting. You could also stand them in a saucer of damp pebbles. Give broad, glossy leaves an occasional wipe with a cloth.

■ Pinching out the tips of some houseplants can encourage them to grow bushier.

■ Keeping flowering plants slightly pot-bound makes them flower more.

■ Avoid placing plants in strong heat or near

Mythbuster!

Popular remedies such as putting copper coins, aspirin, lemonade, or bleach in the water won't do your fresh flowers any favors. In fact, they will do more harm than good.

"How do I make cut flowers last?"

chilly drafts. Many houseplants like to be outdoors in summer but wait until all frosts are over first.

■ Check your plants regularly for signs of stress, pests, or disease. Remove dead leaves and flowers.

Caring for cut flowers

Treat your cut flowers properly and they should repay you with at least a week of blooms and fragrance. Flowers grown commercially are specially treated after cutting, which means that they will last longer than varieties cut from the garden.

Follow these tips for long-lasting cut flowers. Choose blooms with firm petals or with buds that show some color to ensure that the flowers will develop fully.

■ Make sure vases are clean. Bacteria can harm flowers.

■ Use fresh, lukewarm water. There is less oxygen in it, and this helps to stop air bubbles from forming in the stem that will block water uptake. It also encourages some flowers to

open up. However, spring bulb flowers like daffodils and tulips prefer cold water.

■ Strip all leaves below the water level.

■ Take at least 1¼ in (3cm) off all stems, making a slanted cut with a sharp knife to increase the area for taking up water, and stop it from resting on the bottom of the vase and sealing itself. Don't smash or pierce the stems, or use blunt scissors, because this destroys the water vessels and reduces water intake.

■ Change the vase water regularly, and add flower food to reduce bacteria, encourage buds to open, and lengthen the life of the flowers.

■ Don't mix daffodils and narcissi with other flowers—the latex they emit shortens the life of other flowers. You can put daffodils in water for at least 12 hours on their own and then arrange them with other flowers.

■ Don't put flowers near ripening fruit. The

fruit releases tiny amounts of ethylene gas, which prematurely ages flowers. Dying flowers do the same so always remove them promptly from the vase.

■ Don't place flowers in a draft that will chill the flowers, or in bright sunlight, which encourages bacteria to breed. Keep them away from overwarm central heating, too.

Vases

Vases come in all shapes and sizes, giving a great range of ways in which to display your favorite flowers. If your vase is colored or, more importantly, has a design, make sure that it does not clash with your flowers—remember that the flowers are the most important part of the display!

You don't just have to stick to traditional vases—make use of old teapots, water jugs, glass bottles, or earthenware pots. Use anything that will hold water tightly (you can put a plastic bag in the bottom of containers that you suspect may not be up to the job) and is heavy and broad based enough not to fall over.

As a guide, flowers ought to be just over twice the height of the vase. However, you don't have to keep to this. Large-headed blooms, such as roses or camellias, might be cut just below the head and floated in a wide bowl of water. Display tall, thin flowers, such as orchids, tulips, irises, or lilies, in a simple, tall vase. If the vase is very thin, display them in stems of one or two.

If you're buying flowers to fill a large vase, and would like to create an impressive display, use filler flowers and leaves, such as baby's breath, eucalyptus, and ferns to fill space. Make sure that leaves look fresh and are not about to wilt.

Never stop experimenting and being creative with your vases and flower arranging. It often takes a while to get the look you want exactly right, but when you find that you can create lovely displays that your friends marvel at, it'll be worth all the effort.

Emergencies!

Blocked sinks, pipes that freeze, and the occasional flood can affect any of us. So it's helpful to know a few basic remedies for the most common household emergencies to limit the damage before the professionals arrive.

Plumbing

You don't have to be an expert to deal with minor plumbing problems. It helps to have a basic tool kit in an accessible box, which should include an adjustable wrench (spanner), plumber's mate (a sealant "putty" that seals gaps in screw threads), resin, and a plunger.

■ Make sure that you know where to turn off the water in your home, and practice turning it on and off occasionally so you won't get any nasty surprises in an emergency.

■ Buy several spare washers of the right size, and keep them somewhere accessible.

Dripping faucets

There's nothing more annoying—and more wasteful—than a dripping faucet, which can also create a build-up of scale. A dripping faucet may just need a new washer, but it could also hint at something more serious such as a cracked pipe.

To replace a washer, turn off the water to the faucet and unscrew the faucet cover, protecting it with a soft cloth. Unscrew the large nut inside and remove the valve mechanism. Take out the old washer, replace it with a new one and then reassemble the faucet. If you don't have a new one, try flipping the old one over as a short-term measure. If changing washers is beyond you, as a temporary measure you can tie a piece of string to the spout of a dripping faucet to carry the drips quietly into the sink.

Dripping pipes

Burst and dripping pipes can cause floods that wreak havoc with your furnishings and may even bring down ceilings so speedy action is called for when trouble strikes. Always turn off the water at the mains and if it looks serious call in a plumber (check the call-out charge first). If the drip is near a source of electricity, turn off the main power, too.

Quick fixes for cracked pipes

Copper pipes: split a section of garden hose lengthways and slip it over the broken pipe, securing it with hose clips.

Lead and plastic pipes: squeeze petroleum jelly into the crack and bind the pipe with a rag or waterproof tape.

Burst pipes

■ Turn off the main water supply and open all the faucets to drain the system. Remember to close them later so they don't spurt once the supply is restored.

■ Turn off the main electricity supply if water is streaming near light fittings.

■ Switch off the water heater so metal pipes don't overheat.

■ Locate the source of the leak. If possible, bind the crack with an old cloth or some waterproof tape. Keep a bucket under it, and contact a plumber.

■ Accumulated water above a ceiling is very heavy and could bring the ceiling down. If you can locate it, pierce it with a metal skewer or a nail. Place a bucket underneath to catch drips, move furniture and rugs away, and cover carpets.

Problem pipes

Noisy pipes: these are often caused by vibration due to a lack of support. Secure loose pipes by placing foam rubber between them and the walls.

Airlocks: air may get into pipes if a lot of water is suddenly drawn off the system. You can sometimes release the air by tapping gently along the pipes with a mallet that has been wrapped in cloth.

To cure an airlock, turn all faucets on full to run water through the pipes. If this doesn't work, connect a piece of garden hose between a mains faucet and the one that is faulty. Turn on the faulty faucet, then the clear one. The pressure of the mains water should push the air out of the pipe and back into the tank. Turn off the faucets and disconnect the hose when the noise in the pipe stops. Reduce the pressure of the mains water supply to prevent another airlock.

Frozen pipes: to defrost a frozen pipe turn off the mains first. Turn on faucets fed from the frozen pipe to let out any water. Locate the frozen area and hold a hairdryer on a warm (not hot) setting close to the frozen part of the pipe (or wrap it in cloths wrung out in hot water). You can thaw frozen outdoor pipes by pouring hot water around the area of the pipe that is frozen.

Preventing freezing

■ For pipes that tend to freeze regularly, leave cold faucets on slightly overnight during very cold spells in the winter.
■ Put a handful of cooking salt or washing soda down drains last thing at night to prevent pipes from freezing.
■ Insulate pipes using foam secured in place with lagging tape.
■ If you go away on vacation, set your central heating on very low to prevent freezing.

Blocked drains and sinks

Sinks and baths: bale out water in a blocked sink into a bucket. Pour a cupful of washing soda followed by boiling water down the drain, repeating if necessary. If this doesn't work, use a plunger. Smear the rim with petroleum jelly, place it over the drain hole, and run water until the cup is covered. Pump the handle in an up-and-down movement.

Outside drains: use the same treatments for blockages outdoors. It's handy to keep a set of drain rods in case of serious blockages. These are inexpensive and can be found in home renovation retail outlets.

U-bend blockages: you can't clear a blockage in a U-bend with a plunger because of the shape. Instead, place a bucket underneath the bend, and unscrew the U-bend. Carefully poke a piece of sturdy wire, such as a straightened-out coat hanger, up the pipe and maneuver it until you free the blockage.

Blocked toilets

If water rises to the rim and drains slowly, you've got a blocked toilet. This is unpleasant and can also cause flooding.

First, stop flushing the toilet, and let the water drain away as much as possible. Then tip a bucket of water rapidly into the bowl. If it's still blocked, quickly work a toilet plunger up and down in the bowl.

If the cistern is overflowing, you need to keep the ball float-arm upright to prevent more water from flowing in. The easiest way to do this is to tie it to a stick or wooden spoon that will lie across the width of the cistern until you can get a new float arm fixed.

If you suspect your cistern is leaking and wasting water, you can test it by pouring in a little vegetable dye, which will then appear in the toilet if there is a leak. If so, you may need a plumber.

Electrical appliances

Some washing machines and dishwashers may overflow if you use the wrong, or too much, detergent. Set the dial so that the machine begins to empty. Run a rinse cycle with the machine empty before rinsing clothes or crockery to get rid of the excess soap. (Remember to put down old towels on floors to soak up water if the machine continues to leak.) If the detergent is not a problem, check that the filter and soap compartment have been put in properly and are clean. If you cannot see a reason for the overflow, empty the machine, unplug it, and call a plumber. Be sure to turn off electricity if the water is near switches or sockets.

chapter 6

Safety and Security

The First-Aid Magic Box

You can buy first-aid kits from drugstores and supermarkets or you can make up your own and keep it in a specially marked box. Make sure that you have the telephone numbers of emergency services, doctors, and dentists somewhere that can be easily found in an emergency (see page 106).

Always store medicines a box where it is easily accessible to adults but where children cannot reach. Remember to replace used-up and out-of-date items—you could decide to go through your kit every three months, discarding and replenishing. As well as a first-aid kit at home, you may also like to keep one in the car, for emergencies. Some of the basics that it is advisable to stock include:

Antihistamine cream for treating insect bites and stings.
Calamine lotion to relieve the itching of insect bites and rashes.
Dressings such as sterile pads, bandages of various sizes, eye pads and gauze pads.
Adhesive bandages—make sure that you have got a good selection for various needs, and when you use them ensure that you choose one big enough to cover the wound.
Hypoallergenic tape or safety pins for holding bandages and dressings in place.
Tweezers for removing splinters.
Scissors for cutting dressings and bandages.
Spray disinfectant.
Alcohol-free cleansing wipes are ideal for when there's no water available. By using alcohol-free wipes you can reduce the chance of allergic reactions.
Painkillers suitable for children and adults.

Going Green
A tiny bottle of natural lavender oil costs very little but has several uses. It relieves the pain of sunburn and insect bites, acts as an air and clothes freshener as well as repelling moths, and, of course, it can be used in the bath.

The Herbal First-Aid Kit

There are few reliable studies that conclusively prove that herbal remedies work, but for minor conditions natural alternatives are soothing and often make us feel better. For serious conditions always consult a doctor. Some ailments that can be treated by traditional herbal first-aid include:

Minor cuts: apply tincture of calendula (pot marigold) as an antiseptic.

Hangovers: the herb silymarin (milk thistle) is said to protect and restore the liver. Take one or two tablets a day over festive periods. Evening primrose oil can also help to prevent hangovers, but you need to take tablets before drinking (follow dosage instructions on the box).

Indigestion: alfalfa and ginger settle the stomach; peppermint is good for cramps and can be taken as a herbal tea; camomile is anti-inflammatory and can be taken as a soothing tea or tincture.

Insect bites and stings: relieve pain and itching with neat lavender or tea tree oil, or mix 2 drops of either camomile, lavender, or lemon essential oils with 2 tablespoons (30ml) of vegetable carrier oil. Another method is to rub basil leaves on stings. For bee stings apply bicarbonate of soda made into a paste with water.

Other traditional remedies for mosquito and gnat bites or wasp and bee stings include cider vinegar, feverfew, garlic, lemon, or witch hazel. For a natural insect repellent apply diluted citronella, lemon, eucalyptus, or tea tree essential oil to the skin.

Coughs: slice an onion in a bowl, cover with runny honey and leave overnight. The onion juice will seep into the honey. Take a dessert spoonful as needed. For a sweeter alternative a tea made of freshly squeezed lemon juice, hot water, and honey is soothing.

Colds: Add 1–2 tablespoons (15–30ml) of powdered mustard to hot water to create a relaxing foot bath. For a soothing ginger drink slice 1oz (25g) fresh ginger root and add 5 cloves, 2 broken cinnamon sticks, 1 tablespoon of coriander seeds, and 1 pint (500ml) of water. Simmer for 15 minutes. Strain off the herbs and spices, add a squeeze of lemon juice and a teaspoon of honey, and drink.

If you feel a cold coming on, take echinacea tea, tablets, or tincture (tincture is most efficient) to keep it away, and to keep your immune system in good order, .

Bruising: comfrey or arnica can be used as creams or compresses.

Chilblains (unbroken): apply oil of peppermint or rosemary, or soak feet in a bath made from powdered mustard as described above. Gently but thoroughly dry your feet with a towel and put on socks before going to bed.

Minor sunburn: apply neat lavender essential oil directly to the affected area. For a soothing aftersun oil or lotion add 6 drops of bergamot, 6 drops of lavender, 5 drops of camomile, and 5 drops of sandalwood oils to 4 tablespoons (60ml) of carrier oil.

Watch Out for Children

Once babies become mobile their naturally inquisitive nature can get them into trouble fast. A few basic tips will make your home safer and enable you to relax a little. Small children should never be left unattended. Medicines, electrical equipment, and anything sharp or potentially dangerous should always be kept well out of reach. Here are safeguards that you might want to install.

Mesh net: this will discourage a cat from jumping into a baby buggy or crib.

Childproof locks: these can be used on cupboards, windows, appliances, toilets, doors, lids, and openings.

Safety glass: this will not shatter when it is broken and is particularly good for use on internal or patio doors. Alternatively, use self-adhesive safety film to stop glass from shattering when it breaks. Transfers placed on big windows or glass doors are useful to draw children's attention to the fact that the glass is there.

Corner protectors: these can be stuck over sharp corners to cushion in case of bumps.

Stair gate: this will stop your children from falling down the stairs or restrict them to one part of the house.

Fire guard: this prevents a child or animal from getting too close to any kind of open fire.

Stove and hob guards: these stop children from reaching up and pulling saucepans down

Socket guards: these fit into electrical sockets and prevent children from poking things into them. Some double as a nightlight.

Electrical lead guards: these secure trailing leads to a wall or can be used to bundle trailing cords neatly together. If you're replacing appliances, choose ones with coiled safety leads.

Avoiding Accidents

Simple precautions can prevent accidents and even save lives. It's worth supplementing these by taking a professionally run first-aid course.

- Accidents tend to happen most frequently in kitchens and bathrooms. Always mop up spills so nobody slips, especially on tiled floors.
- Attach a safety rail to the wall by the bath if you live with elderly or infirm members of the family.
- Turn the handle of pots and pans away from the edge of the stove and keep children away from hot oven doors.
- Store matches out of reach.
- Replace ordinary glass panels fitted into doors with safety glass.
- Always use a fireguard.
- Secure loose rugs or mats with nonslip pads or tape.
- Install good lighting in busy thoroughfares, such as hallways and staircases.
- Always switch off an electric iron if you have to answer the door or telephone.

Fire precautions

Experts recommend installing smoke detectors near every bedroom and living room and having at least one on each floor. Alarms are inexpensive and simple to install.

Make sure that your family knows what to do in the event of a fire, including escape routes and meeting places.

Don't buy secondhand, used furniture filled with polyurethane foam that is not fire retardant. If this catches fire it burns rapidly and gives off toxic fumes.

Other good fire-safety items to have in the home are a fire blanket and fire extinguisher.

Emergencies

Keep a list of essential numbers next to the telephone, and written instructions in case the caller panics. Numbers should include:

- Fire, police, and ambulance
- Doctor and dentist
- The nearest hospital with an ER
- Close family members, both home and work
- Pharmacist that is open late at night and on weekends
- Emergency utility numbers, such as electricity, gas, and water
- Taxi service

The Household Genie's Tip

Use anti-slip matting underneath rugs on hard flooring to stop them from sliding around, and for rugs on carpets, stick pieces of Velcro at the corners to keep them in place.

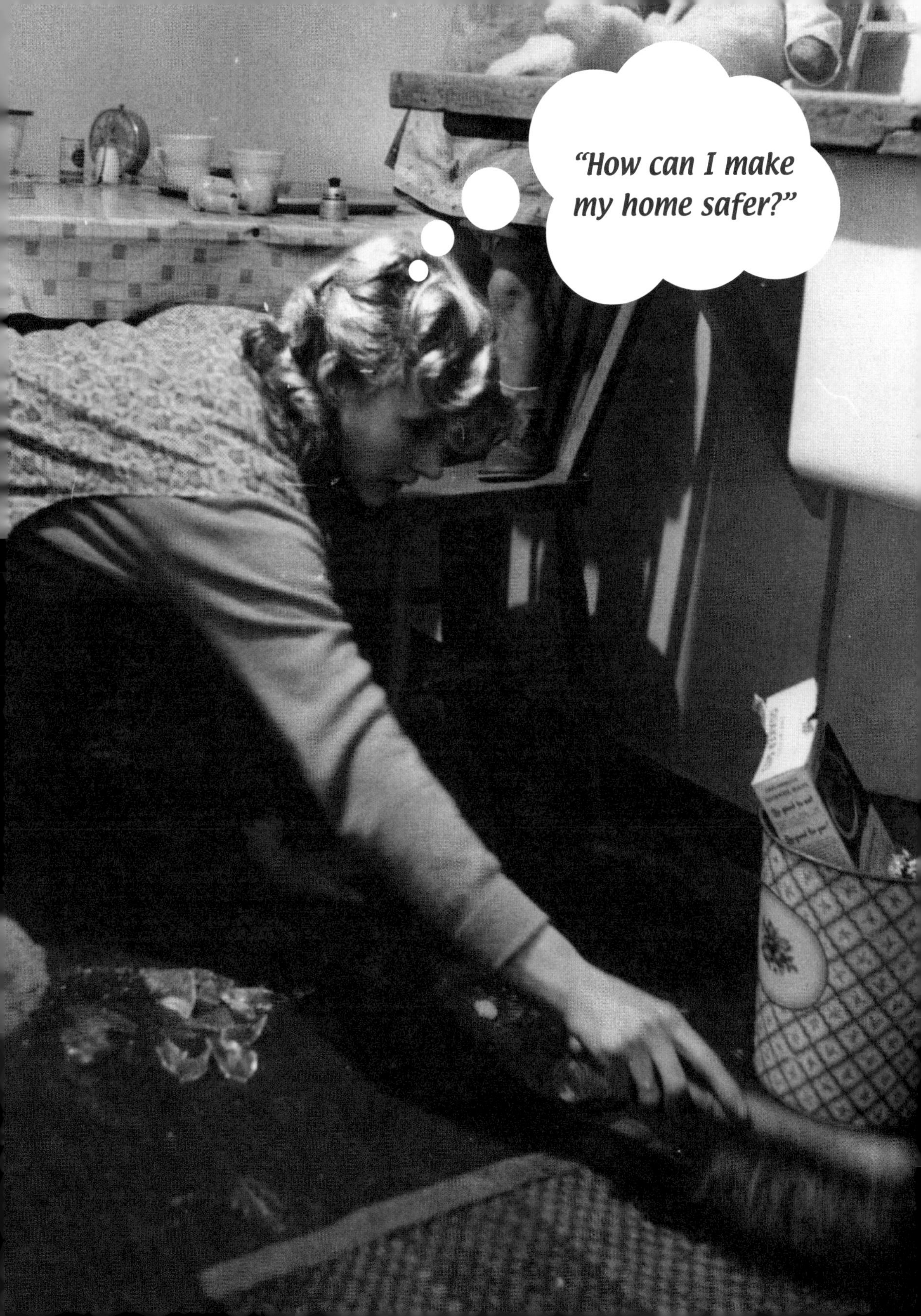
"How can I make my home safer?"

Feel Safe and Secure at Home

Many burglaries could have been prevented. Most are committed by passing thieves who spot an opportunity. Frequently they do not even have to force an entry thanks to a door or window conveniently left open. Burglars like easy pickings—they don't like wrestling with locked windows or doors. They are especially averse to security deadlocks on doors because they can't open them even from the inside, which means they must escape through a window. So check the security of your home, and strengthen any weak spots as soon as possible. A small outlay will make your home more secure, buy you peace of mind, and may even result in lower home insurance costs.

The basics

Burglar alarms: visible burglar alarms make burglars think twice.

Gates and fences: a high wall or fence at the back of a house can discourage a burglar. Check for weak spots where a thief could get in. A thorny hedge along a boundary can also be a strong deterrent. Make sure that the front of the house is still visible to passers-by, so that a burglar can't work unseen.

Small windows: even small windows such as casement windows, skylights, or bathroom fanlights need locks—a thief can get in through any gap larger than a human head.

Front door roof: an agile thief could reach first-floor windows from this roof, so install solid window locks that need a key.

Garages and sheds: never leave a garage or garden shed unlocked, especially if it has a connecting door to the house. Lock tools and ladders away so that a thief cannot use them to break into your house.

Apartments

Make sure that your front door is strong. It should be as strongly built as the main outside door of the building. Fit hinge bolts; these stop someone from pulling the door from its hinges. And insert a special steel strip into the doorframe to prevent the chub lock from

Mythbuster!

Don't be caught out by hiding spare keys in under a flowerpot or doormat. A thief will look there first. Professional thieves know all the tricks, so entrust keys to a close friend or neighbor.

STOP THIEF!

Strangers at the door

The best defenses against a dubious caller are a viewer or spy hole in the door and a strong door chain. Always make sure that unknown callers are who they say they are, and ask to see an ID card. Check their identification by ringing their employer.

Burglar alarms and safes

If you have lots of valuable possessions or you live in an area with a high burglary rate, you should consider a burglar alarm or a safe. Ranging from inexpensive do-it-yourself kits to pricey, sophisticated systems, there are numerous burglar alarms on the market. High-quality alarms fitted by a specialist will certainly be a deterrent to burglars. If self-assembly isn't your thing, easy-to-install wire-free alarms have sensors fitted around the house that transmit radio detection signals to a control system. Do get expert advice and a number of quotes. Consult your insurance company for the specialists they recommend.

Lighting

Good lighting deters thieves. Some exterior lights have light sensors or an infrared sensor that switches the light on temporarily when it detects something in its range. These can be either wired into your system or run on batteries. You can also buy sensors to convert an existing outdoor light into a security type.

being forced open. If you have a telephone entry system, don't let strangers in or prop the door open.

Side passage

Thieves like working at the back of a house where there is less chance of being seen, so fit a strong, high gate across the passage. If you share an alleyway with a neighbor, discuss sharing the cost.

Doors

If your front and back doors are not strong and safe, neither is your home. Make sure that the doors themselves are strong and

HOW SAFE ARE YOUR WINDOWS?

Windows

Home renovation retail outlets sell inexpensive key-operated locks to fit all kinds of window, and these are useful deterrents to thieves who don't want to break windows and attract attention. Secure vulnerable windows such as ground-floor windows, windows that can't be seen from the street, and windows that can be reached from a drainpipe or flat roof. If crime is a real problem in your area, think about using laminated-glass or security grilles.

Patio doors

Patio doors are particularly vulnerable so seek specialist advice on fitting locks at top and bottom. Install an anti-lift device to stop a thief from lifting the door off its rail. Fit security mortise locks to french doors, and mortise bolts to top and bottom of both doors.

solid, at least 2 in (5cm) thick. Glass panels are especially vulnerable. Door viewers enable you to see who callers are.

Fit a five-lever mortise deadlock to front and back doors that can only be opened with a key (don't leave the key in the lock). With this a thief cannot smash a nearby glass panel to open the door from the inside. Remember to keep your spare keys in a secure, hard-to-find place so that if the thief enters the property through a window they can't then carry your belongings out through the door.

If you are thinking about installing a PVC door, check with the manufacturer that a door chain will be fitted. It can be difficult and expensive to have a chain installed on an existing PVC door.

Steps to a safer home

Bear these tips in mind to keep your home safe from intruders.

- Always buy the best level of security you can afford.
- With all security think about the risk of fire, and means of escape. Fit a smoke detector.
- Never leave a key in or near the lock, or where it might be visible to a thief.
- If in doubt, ask for advice from a reputable locksmith or from the crime prevention officer at your local police station.
- Use marker pens to imprint your property with your name and zip code.
- Don't place your TV or video near a window.
- Draw the curtains if you are going out for the evening, and leave a light on.

■ Always ask to see the identity details of someone claiming to be from gas, electricity, water, or telephone service providers. Genuine staff always carry a recognizable form of photo-identity card for you to scrutinize.

If you are going away

■ Cancel any newspapers or milk deliveries well in advance.

■ Get a friend or neighbor to look after your home when you are on vacation. Ask them to collect mail left in the letterbox, adjust the curtains, sweep up leaves, tidy the lawn and generally make the house look lived in.

■ Use timed light switches, set to come on during the evening while you are away. Use timed switches on radios to create the impression that someone is in the house.

■ If you have a telephone answering machine,

The Household Genie's Tip

You can grow prickly shrubs around your house as deterrents to thieves. But bear in mind that high hedges can be helpful to burglars, especially at the front. They conceal broken windows and suspicious activities from people passing by.

don't leave a message saying you're away.

■ Don't advertise your absence when you're on holiday, or even out at work or shopping.

You're not expecting fire?...

...tomorrow 1,000 like you will experience their first!

chapter 7

Laundry and Clothes Care

Wash Day Magic

Washing clothes is a necessary evil, but the better your system the longer your clothes will last. Look after your clothes and bedding well and they'll stay fresh and colorfast for years. Modern washing machines, dryers, and irons are superefficient and make life easier. All you have to do is prepare everything in a systematic way to maximize your appliances' performance.

Detergents, especially biological types, are powerful, so use only as much as is recommended on the pack. Otherwise, your clothes will fade and weaken quickly. Follow garment-care label instructions and remove your laundry as soon as the cycle has finished to prevent overcreasing and mildew, especially in warm weather.

Machine-washing

- Go through all the pockets to check for pens, coins, tissues, etc.—they won't do your machine or laundry any favors. Turn all pockets outward.
- Brush off any surplus mud, dust, or fluff.
- Close zippers and do up all buttons so they don't snap, and to prevent damage to your machine.
- Turn pile fabrics, jeans, and corduroy fabrics inside out.
- Pin pairs of socks together with safety pins to prevent that mysterious "single sock" syndrome.
- Mend holes, tears, and loose buttons in clothes beforehand so that damage already there doesn't get worse as clothes are tossed around in the machine.
- Organize to wash clothes with the same wash symbol together.

- If you have to machine-wash mixed loads, put them through the most delicate cycle on their labels.

Conserve energy

For more energy-saving strategies see Simple tips on page 91.
- Shake items out before loading, and load one at a time to reduce tangling.
- Load evenly with small items, then large, taking care not to overfill the machine. Front loaders should be filled loosely to the top of the agitator—front loaders

The Household Genie's Tip

To remove soap and cut down on rinsing time when hand washing, add 1 tablespoon (15ml) of white vinegar or some talcum powder to the final rinse.

are too full if you can't reach to the back of the drum without meeting obstruction.

■ Consider paying a little more for an energy-efficient model when buying a new washing machine. You'll end up paying lower fuel bills in the long run.

■ Wash maximum loads when you can, or use the half-load option for smaller loads to cut down on energy waste.

■ Set your machine at a lower temperature for lightly soiled loads.

■ Rinse with cold water when hand washing.

■ Use high-spin speeds before tumble drying (except for synthetic fabrics).

■ Buy refill packs of detergents and fabric conditioners. Use the correct quantities stated on the packet—don't guess. Try to buy environmentally friendly products.

Pre-wash treatment

Remove stains from clothes prior to washing, since laundering may cause marks to set. Use pre-wash sprays or sticks, or soak items in

Going Green

Brighten up yellowing cotton items by soaking them in hot water and a cupful of lemon juice rather than household bleach. If you must use bleach, always dilute an egg cupful to a bucketful of cold water. Wear rubber gloves and read the garment care label. Fabrics such as wool, silk, and viscose should not be bleached. You can also use borax and even bicarbonate of soda.

biological detergent if the fabric is suitable. Or you could try some of our "green" tips below.

■ Fabrics that don't usually benefit from soaking include silk, wool, leather, elastane (Lycra), anything that has been specially treated with flame retardant, easy-care, and ones with noncolorfast dyes.

■ Soak soiled clothing in a plastic bucket or basin with plenty of water. Check that the detergent is thoroughly dissolved before adding the clothes.

■ Water should be cool for protein-based stains such as egg, blood, and milk, and hand hot for others.

■ Leave to soak for several hours, or overnight for whites.

■ With new, noncolorfast clothes, you can reduce color loss by soaking them in a solution of salt and water using I tablespoon (15ml) of salt to I pint (500ml) of water.

Care of washing machines

■ Clean your washing machine occasionally by running it empty on a hot cycle with a little white vinegar in the detergent compartment. This will clear any soap deposits.

■ Use the correct amount of detergent. Using too little won't give good results, but too much will not rinse out clothes properly.

■ Clean out filters regularly. If they become completely blocked, the drum will not turn.

Hand washing

■ Sort your laundry according to color and temperature and wash like with like.

■ Make sure the detergent or soap flakes are thoroughly dissolved.

Fabric Care Symbols

Washing *The number in the wash tub shows the most effective washing temperature.*

Cotton Wash *(no bar)*
A wash tub without a bar indicates that normal (maximum) washing conditions may be used at the appropriate temperature.

Synthetics Wash *(single bar)*
A single bar beneath the wash tub indicates reduced (medium) washing conditions at the appropriate temperature.

Wool Wash *(broken bar)*
A broken bar beneath the wash tub indicates much reduced (minimum) washing conditions, and is designed specifically for machine washable wool products.

Hand Wash Only
Wash by hand

Bleaching

Chlorine Bleach may be used

Do not use Chlorine Bleach.

Ironing *Steaming may be beneficial to remove unwanted creasing.*

Hot Iron

Warm Iron

Cool Iron

Dry Cleaning

Must be professionally dry-cleaned.
The letters contained within the circle and/or a bar beneath the circle will indicate the solvent and the process to be used by the dry-cleaner.

Do not dry-clean.

Tumble Drying *A cross through any symbol means "DO NOT".*

May be tumble dried:

With low heat setting.

With high heat setting.

Do not tumble dry.

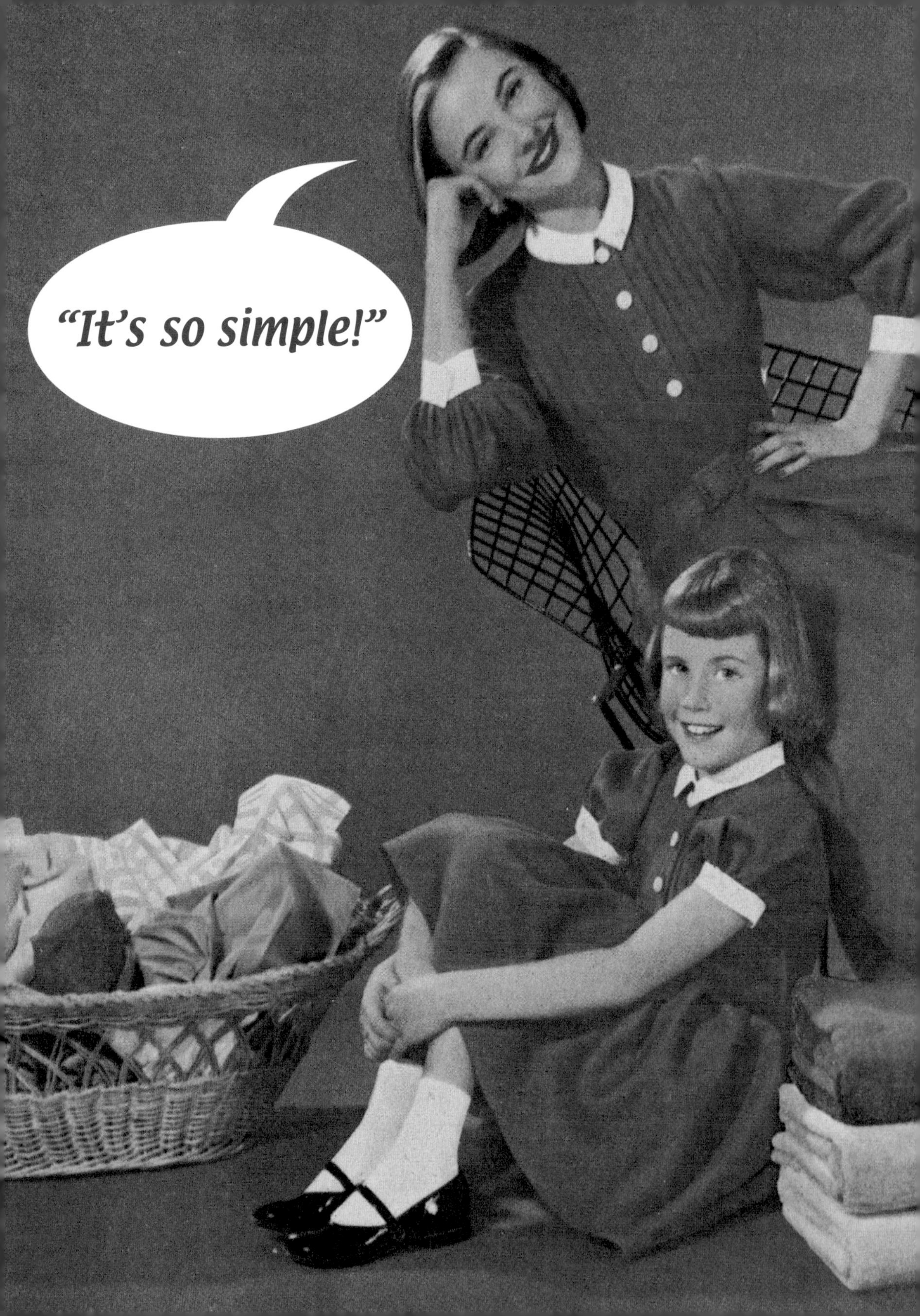
"It's so simple!"

- Rinse several times in cold water until it is free of soap scum. Add a little vinegar to the final rinse to remove all the suds.

- If you're washing woolen items, gently squeeze the water through them. Don't rub the clothing because this will make the fibers mat together.

- Don't allow items to stretch as you lift them out of the water.

Care of bulky or delicate items

For more about special items see Textiles on page 8.

Silk: add two lumps of sugar to the rinse water to give silk body or a little lanolin to protect and restore the fibers. **Pillows:** reverse the pillows each time that you make the bed to reduce wear on one side. If you must wash pillows, do it in the bath, using a soap-flake

solution and rinsing thoroughly.

Small or delicate items: launder items such as lace or tights in a pillowcase to prevent them from snagging and tangling.

Quilts: quilts and duvets are usually too heavy to wash in domestic machines, and are too large to be washed by hand easily. Sponge off any spills and stains immediately, then take them to a launderette or to a professional cleaner. If you have them dry-cleaned, it's important to hang them somewhere outside for several hours to get rid of the highly toxic fumes that linger inside the thick interior.

Sheets: after laundering place white linen or cotton sheets at the bottom of the pile in the linen cupboard. Regular rotation and use will prevent sheets from yellowing.

Drying Clothes can be this Easy!

Dry clothes properly and you'll need to spend less time on ironing and folding. Hang clothes outside whenever the weather permits. This will save electricity, and is gentler on clothes than tumble drying. Strong sunlight can cause fading, so don't hang colored items directly in bright summer sunlight. When hanging items on the line, try to keep seams and creases in the right places.

Clothes made from delicate fabrics should always be dried flat. Roll them in a towel to remove excess moisture, then stretch them gently into shape, and leave them to dry on a new, thick, dry towel. To reshape stretched cuffs on woolen sweaters, dip them in hot water, then dry them with a hairdryer. If you don't have access to an outside line, use a drying rack in a well-aired room or on a balcony, but don't dry clothes over a heater or radiator.

Drying tips
Line drying:
- Wipe the line before use.
- Dry whites out on a line whenever possible because the sunlight will bleach and freshen up their whiteness.
- Hang pleated garments on a hanger.
- Hang drip-dry skirts by the waistband.
- Turn colored garments inside out to prevent them from fading.
- Fold sheets in half and hang them from the line by the hem.
- Hang striped garments vertically.
- Do not hang silk, wool, or polyamide outside to dry. The sunlight will cause them to yellow and weaken.

Drying different items
Sweaters: a synthetic or wool sweater can be dried hanging from a clothes line by threading a pair of old panty hose (tights) through the armholes and pegging them at the wrist and neck holes to support the garment.

"How do I line-dry a sweater?"

T-shirts: peg these from the bottom or place on a hanger to minimize the cotton knit of T-shirts pulling in different directions.

Trousers: hang trousers from the bottom or hems on the inside legs, or drape over trouser hangers before hanging on the line.

Shirts: hang shirts on a hanger and peg it to the line to stop it from blowing away.

Stockings and panty hose (tights): clip clothes pegs to the feet to prevent them from blowing around and tangling or snagging.

Socks: peg pairs of socks on a hanger to save space, or use a special space-saving round hanger with small pegs.

Sheets: peg the sheet at both ends first, then peg each side halfway along to make a billowing bag shape that allows the air to circulate and help the sheets to dry faster.

Using a tumble dryer

- Spin dry clothes first unless the label advises you not to.
- Do not tumble dry wool, knitted clothing, delicates, or elastanes.
- Choose the right program for the type of fabric. If you dry synthetics at too high a temperature, they could melt, crease, or shrink.
- Do not run a tumble dryer for longer than required. This wastes energy and overdries the clothes, which makes ironing harder.
- Don't overload the dryer—it won't work properly. Leave room at the top of the drum so the clothes can move around freely.
- Tumble drying can cause static to build up, so use a fabric conditioner with each wash.
- Use cloths impregnated with fabric softener in the tumble dryer to avoid creasing.

Mythbuster!

A line of brightly colored clothes fluttering on a washing line is a picture-postacrd ideal of washing-day efficiency, but in fact strong sunlight can fade colored garments. Such garments should be hung in the shade or indoors during the summer.

Fresh Ideas for Ironing

Freshly ironed clothes look beautiful and feel nice to wear. Ironing also has a practical side because pressed clothing and bedding are much easier to fold and store flat, so they take up less room. Ironing is easiest if clothes are slightly damp. It makes sense to build in time for an ironing session soon after washing and drying. You can keep ironing to a minimum by hanging up or folding clothes as soon as they come out of the tumble dryer, and by hanging damp clothes on hangers so they retain their shape.

■ Iron acrylic or fabrics with a slightly raised nap on the reverse side to avoid making them shiny. Or press them using a pressing cloth (this is a clean tea towel or piece of cut-up sheet placed over the fabric). The cloth can be dampened if necessary.

■ Always iron bulky fabrics such as denim and canvas inside out, particularly if the fabric is dark, in order to avoid fabric shine, particularly on thick seams.

■ Big items such as sheets, duvet covers, and tablecloths can be folded into manageable rectangles and then ironed in sections. You can stop sheets from trailing on the floor by putting the ironed half over a chair back, but cover wooden chairs with an old towel so that any wood coloring doesn't get onto the linen.

■ With silk, iron the reverse of the garment damp using a pressing cloth (see above). Place embroidered silk face down onto a white towel, then press it on the reverse side to make the embroidery stand out.

■ Fine pleats should be ironed in sections; wide pleats should be ironed individually. Use hairpins to keep pleats firmly in place. Take the hairpins out when you come to iron the waistband and hem.

■ If items have trimmings that need a cooler setting than the main fabric, for instance nylon lace on a cotton dress, iron these first, before ironing the rest of the garment.

■ If you often need to iron ties make a rough tie-shaped cardboard template that can be

IRON TEMPERATURE CHART	
Material	**Method**
Cotton and linen	Fairly damp, use hot iron
Rayon	Fairly damp, only warm iron. Don't sprinkle as this causes "grease" spots
Man-made fabrics, nylon, orlon and terylene	Just damp, cool iron
Tussore, shantung	Dry, warm iron on wrong side
Other silks	Slightly damp, warm iron
Wool and wool mixtures	Nearly dry, warm iron

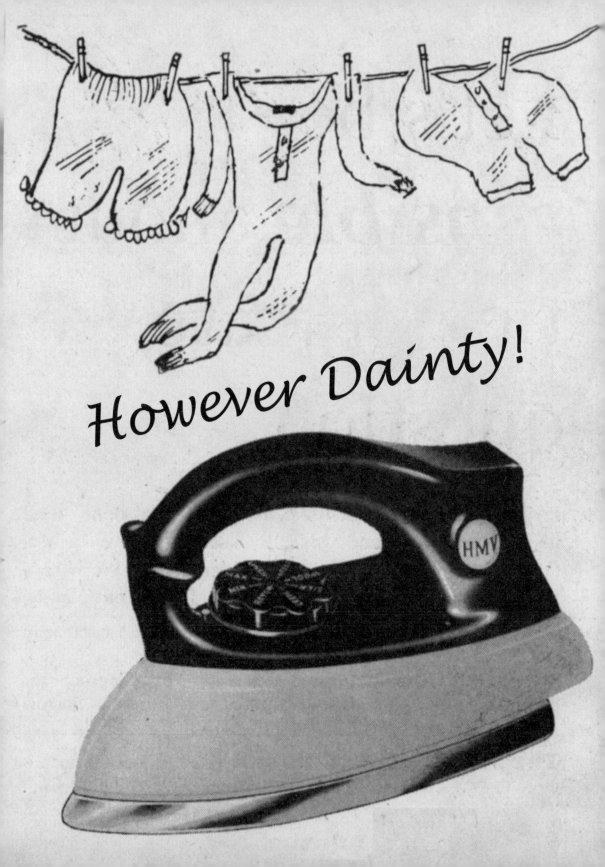

However Dainty!

slipped inside when ironing to stop the seams from showing through.

■ Use a spray bottle to dampen dry clothes. Alternatively, put all the clothes into the tumble dryer with a wet towel, and run the dryer on a no-heat program for a few minutes.

Ironing tips

Before ironing any fabric, check the care-label guide and then set the iron temperature accordingly. Iron items that need the coolest setting first, then work up to the hottest setting. Iron in loads, because irons use up a lot of electricity heating up. Ensure that all items are evenly damp.

■ Clean an iron while it is still warm, but unplugged. Rub it on an old piece of towel to remove stickiness, then, using a damp cloth, rub it with bicarbonate of soda or a proprietary cleaner for sole plates. Wipe with a clean, damp cloth.

■ If you are away from home and don't have access to an iron, hang creased clothes in a steamy bathroom or sprinkle water over them and hang up for a couple of hours to encourage the creases to drop out.

■ Using padded hangers will prevent shoulder marks from appearing on delicate fabrics.

■ Iron around—not over—zippers and buttons. Metal zippers could otherwise

Going Green

Maximize energy by placing aluminum foil under ironing-board covers to reflect heat (or you can buy covers that do this).

How to Iron a Shirt

Begin by ironing double parts, like yoke, front opening, all seams, first on the inside and then on the outside

Iron cuffs on both sides, wrong side first, stretching carefully and smoothing all fullness toward the edges

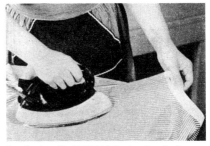

Iron fronts, with shirt laid flat out on board, after you have done the back, taking particular care of pleats

Fold buttoned shirt with shirt tail over cuffs, then double up to form a rectangle, with the front to the outside

damage the iron, and nylon zippers and buttons could melt. Cover metal, mother-of-pearl, or plastic buttons with a spoon to stop the heat of the iron damaging them.

■ To avoid creating a line over seams and hems, iron the garment inside out just up to the seam or hem line.

■ Iron delicate fabrics over a clean, smooth cloth to avoid damaging the fabric.

■ Always iron collars on both sides, wrong side first. Iron inward from the point to avoid pushing any creases to the tip.

■ Use an adjustable ironing board that suits your height, to prevent backache.

Starching

Starching clothes and bed linen makes them crisp. It is especially worth it for linens and formal cotton clothes.

■ If you want a very stiff result, use a powdered starch in a bucket.

■ Spray starch is easier to use but starch lasts longer. Spray on the right side, once the item is dry and just before it is ironed.

Taking Good Care of your Clothes

Keep your clothes in good condition by looking after them and they will last longer and look newer, too. Hang them properly after you take them off. Brush, remove stains, and make any repairs before wearing again. Avoid wearing clothes or shoes two days in a row.

For more about sewing and clothes repair see Sewing Magic in the Good Housekeeping chapter on pages 83–84.

Storing clothes

Storing and hanging clothes properly is essential to keep them looking good. After wearing clothes hang them to air for a few hours before putting them in a cupboard. Remove lint and fluff from clothes with a piece of adhesive tape wrapped around one finger, or with a clean, damp sponge. Don't overcrowd your closets because clothes can't air properly and will become creased and stale. Make a little space by storing out-of-season clothes elsewhere.

Drawer storage: fold clothes across their width. Gravity will help horizontal creases to drop out more quickly than lengthways ones.

Scarves: roll silk scarves around cardboard tubes from aluminum foil or plastic wrap to stop them from creasing.

Nonslip hangers: you can stop clothes from slipping off wire hangers by winding two or three rubber bands around the ends.

Suede: clean fluff off suede accessories and dark clothes by rubbing them with a piece of velvet fabric.

Hats: store hats in cardboard boxes, stuffed with acid-free tissue paper.

Linen closets: store fragrant, unwrapped soap in linen cupboards to scent the contents.

Suitcase storage: put one or two sugar lumps in your empty suitcase to absorb smells when you get back from a vacation.

Moths

Moths thrive in dust and dirt, so before you store clothes or bedding clean them and air them well. Clean out wardrobes, clothes closets, cupboards, and drawers regularly. Natural moth deterrents include dried citrus peel, eucalyptus oil, cloves, and lavender sachets. For large items such as bed linen a few hours hung in bright sunlight should get rid of moths, or put the linen through a tumble-dryer cycle.

Shoe care

Get the most from your shoes by cleaning and polishing them frequently, airing them after wearing and using shoe trees to maintain their

Going Green
Bicarbonate of soda is a natural deodorizer, so sprinkle a little into shoes that smell. Leave this overnight, then shake it out.

The Household Genie's Tip

Charcoal briquettes and chalk sticks absorb damp from clothes closets. Place several in a nylon netting bag or something similar and hang them inside.

"How do I keep my clothes looking good?"

shape. Use a soft brush to apply polish and a duster to give a good shine. Leaving polish on overnight, then buffing in the morning will help the polish nurture the leather.

Canvas shoes: clean dirty canvas shoes with a toothbrush dipped in carpet shampoo. Treat new ones with fabric protector.

Patent shoes: rub these with petroleum jelly and buff them well to achieve a shiny finish.

Leather shoes: coat new leather soles with castor oil or linseed oil to preserve them.

Suede shoes: protect these with a water- or stain-repellent and brush with a plastic or rubber-tipped brush to restore the nap and remove dirt.

Shoe storage:

■ Store your shoes and boots away from direct sunlight to stop them from fading and

cracking, including rubber boots, which may perish. Touch up scuffs on shoes with a matching felt-tip pen or a wax crayon.

■ Wet shoes and boots will dry faster if you stuff them with newspaper. Tight shoes can be stretched a little if you cram them with wet newspaper and leave them overnight. Improvise boot trees by stuffing rolls of newspaper into your boots or shoes to help them keep their shape.

■ Let muddy shoes dry thoroughly but don't leave them next to a hot, open fire or heater, which may crack the leather. Scrape off the mud with a spatula or piece of wood. Sponge any marks with a damp cloth, and stuff with newspaper or shoe trees to keep in shape.

■ If you run out of shoe polish, try using a similarly colored furniture polish instead.

chapter 8

Entertaining

How to Host a Great Children's Party

Children's parties are notoriously hectic, but thorough planning should prepare you for the invasion.

Approach a party like a general before a campaign, devising winning strategies and tactics to ensure success.

■ If you want to stay sane and prevent full-scale hysteria and total chaos, don't invite every single child in the kindergarten class or nursery school. The younger the ages, the fewer the children.

■ Young children have short attention spans, so keep the party to 90 minutes for little children and no more than two or two-and-a-half hours for older children. Keep each activity/game to 5 or 10 minutes at a time.

■ Children's parties work best when there's a (flexible) timetable of events to follow, preferably written down.

■ With small children avoid loud or rough games because they will become overexcited and hard to control.

■ Older children generally delight in theme or activity parties, and can also enjoy the responsibility of helping with the preparations.

■ If you're not very confident around children, bring in professional entertainment. Or bribe a couple of energetic teenagers to take on the role if your funds don't stretch that far.

■ It helps if you can have a few adults on hand to take kids to the bathroom, hand out food, mop up spills, and so on. Remember to provide plenty of snacks and drinks for helpers.

■ One person should be responsible for games, with someone else to help with music and giving out prizes.

■ If you're giving prizes for games, it's nice if everyone wins something, even if it's just some candy.

■ Keep the action to just one area of the house, and make it clear from the beginning which rooms are out of bounds.

■ For younger children, food should be of the finger variety—small sausages, cherry tomatoes, cheese cubes, and chicken drumsticks. Sticks of carrot, celery, and cucumber are all good bets. Avoid food that needs cutlery to save on mess, and use unbreakable, disposable plates. Don't wildly over-cater—much of the food will end up on the floor in any case.

■ In these times of increasing food allergies, it's safer to avoid serving food with nuts in, such as peanut butter sandwiches, unless you're absolutely certain that no-one at the party has such allergies. You might considering mentioning this on invitations.

■ If you're handing out goodie bags at the end, try to make them all exactly the same to avoid arguments.

■ Allow a full 10 minutes before pick-up time for kids to put on shoes and coats, and collect their goodie bags.

Hostess with the Mostess – the Formal Meal

Work out a timetable leading up to the meal, and make a full list of everything you'll need. If you're planning a sit-down dinner, don't invite more people than can sit comfortably around your table.

- Only have place names if you're confident that your guests will enjoy mixing with people they may not know.
- Don't be overambitious and attempt to cook something new. Stick to tried-and-tested dishes. If it will make you feel more confident, try cooking your menu a couple of times in the weeks before your party, timing how long everything takes to prepare and cook.
- Unless you're a very confident host/cook, it helps if even one course—or more—can be prepared in advance. A cold appetizer course, such as a salad or salmon, is a good option. Casseroles can be prepared a day in advance.

- Find out beforehand whether people are vegetarian or have special dietary needs.
- If guests bring a bottle of wine, by all means open it if it's suitable for the meal—if

Flowers

Having flowers on your table is a lovely idea. Keep arrangements small, however, so they don't dominate the setting or stop people from seeing each other through the foliage. Or you can move the arrangement elsewhere when your guests sit down. Also avoid flowers (or candles) with a very strong scent that might clash with your food.

For more about flowers, see Caring for cut flowers on page 96.

Place settings

The days of a battery of implements for different kinds of food are mostly long gone which makes life considerably easier when it comes to laying the table.

Plates: allow a generously proportioned main course plate, with a smaller one to the left for bread.

Cutlery: the general rule of thumb is to work from the outside in according to the order you intend to eat in. Knives, with the blades pointing to the left, should go on the right, along with a soupspoon if needed, while forks go on the left. A dessertspoon and fork can go top to tail above the plate. It's nice to include a smaller knife on a separate bread plate to the left of your setting.

Glasses: these should go above the plate to the right. You should have separate glasses for white wine (smallish), red wine (a bit bigger), beer, and water.

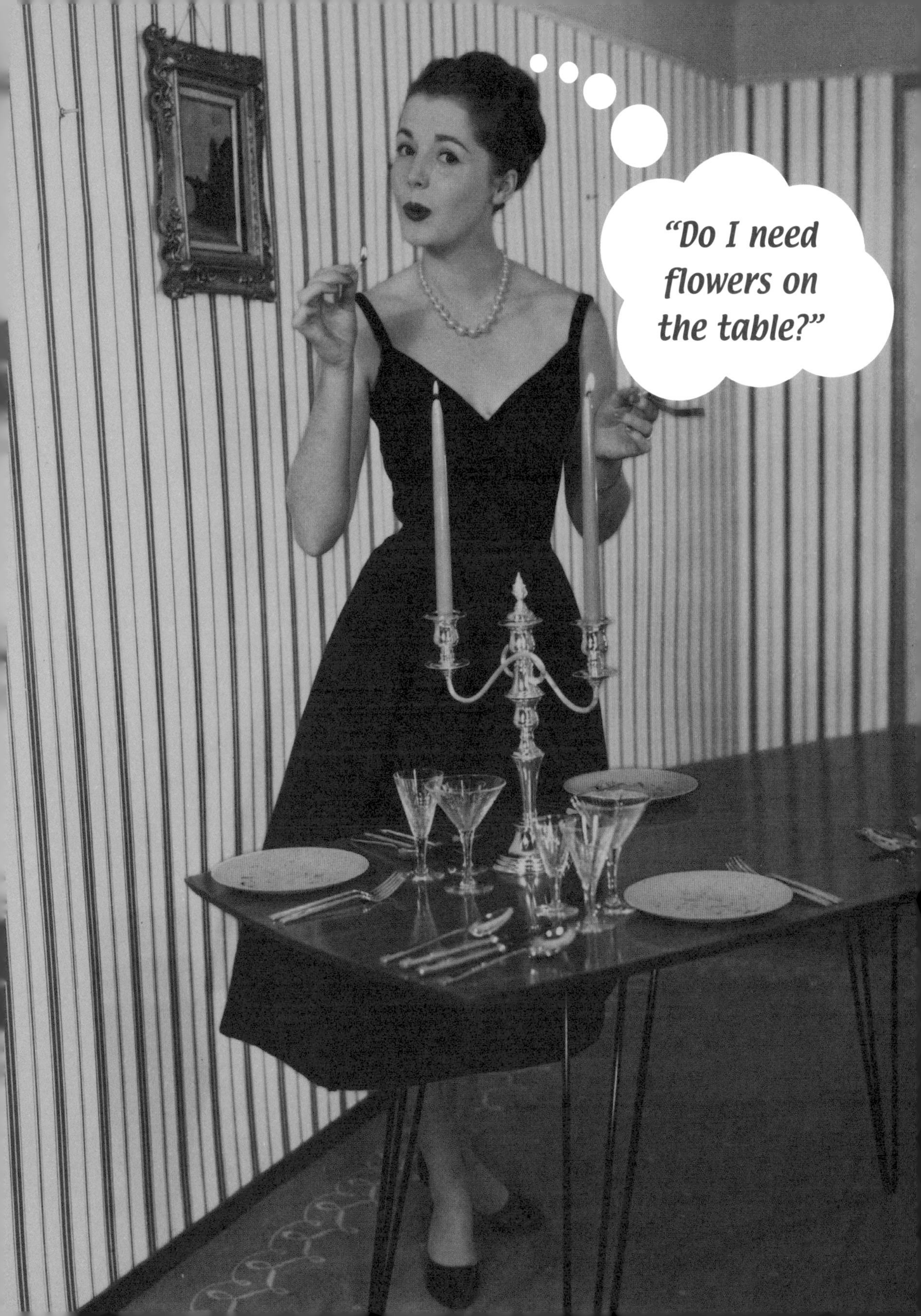
"Do I need flowers on the table?"

not, say that you will save it for another time.

■ Make sure that you have somewhere for people to leave their coats.

■ Ensure that you have a clear smoking policy for guests, for example only in the garden.

■ If you're serving drinks before dinner, either serve snacks or keep the interval before dining quite short. This means people won't be drinking too much on an empty stomach.

Ensure that there is plenty to drink that is nonalcoholic and low-calorie, too.

■ If you really don't enjoy cooking, buy some delicious ready-prepared food and dress it up with exotic salsas and relishes and easy-to-prepare salads and vegetables. Serve with some cheese or nutty bread. You can find most of what you need at a good supermarket, and it will free you from anxiety.

TABLE ETIQUETTE
DO'S AND DON'TS FOR GOOD MANNERS

The hostess should plan the seating of her guests well in advance so that when the party enters the dining-room, she can indicate where each guest is to sit.

As a general rule, guests should be seated with the men and women alternating round the table. If possible, avoid placing husbands and wives side-by-side.

The most important guests are placed at the right and left of the host and hostess, the men near the hostess the women near the host.

The guests should be served in order of importance, the women first. The hostess and the host are the last to be served.

The guests should wait until everyone is served and the hostess has started, before beginning to eat.

The hostess should try to keep the conversation going in a light and pleasant vein.

The guests should avoid getting involved in a heated political discussion and keep off any subject that might offend anyone pres-

ent. It is the height of bad manners to create an awkward situation when your hostess is trying hard to keep a happy and easy atmosphere.

The hostess should do her best to draw into the conversation any shy guest who seems to have little to say.

The guests should pay equal attention to their neighbors on either side.

The hostess should see to it that she is the last to finish a course, so that her guests should not feel that they are holding up the service.

The guests should remember to compliment the hostess on her meal in appreciation of the time and trouble she has taken preparing it.

The hostess should rise at the end of the meal and, if coffee is to follow, say where it will be served.

The guests should leave their napkins, unfolded, by the side of their plates, when they leave the dining room.

COURSE-BY-COURSE

Soup . . . the plate should be tipped away from you when drinking soup.

Meat, fish, chicken . . . bones must not be picked up with your fingers.

Salad . . . should not be transferred from the side plate to the main plate, eat it with its own fork or the same fork and knife provided with the main dish.

Bread . . . rolls should be crumbled, not cut. Leave bread on plate provided.

Wine . . . a little should be poured into the host's glass first, to see whether it is corked.

Coffee . . . after a formal dinner is served in the sitting-room.

An Informal Get-Together

It may be a special occasion such as a birthday, graduation, or anniversary, or you may simply feel like throwing a party for fun, but whatever the case, you need to create the right mood for the occasion. Factors you will have to balance include the reason for the event, your likely guests, and, of course, your budget. Then you need to decide on the music or entertainment or perhaps a theme.

Top tips

- Send out invitations a month or more in advance, especially during festive periods, to make sure your guests will be free on that day. Ask them to reply so you may know how many guests you will be catering for.
- Write a "to do" list. Get as much done in advance as you can, including arranging for the music and any entertainment, food preparation, organizing drinks, glass hire, decoration, your outfit, and so on.
- When calculating the number of guests you'd like to invite, think carefully about the amount of space you have available. Will they all fit into your home or would you be better off hiring a venue?
- Using your backyard or even setting up a marquee gives you extra space; it can be used instead of the house to avoid carpets or furniture being ruined.
- Make clear to guests whether you would like them to bring a bottle or not.
- Accept all offers of help—you'll need them.
- Roll up carpets and rugs and clear away furniture if there's going to be dancing.
- Tell the neighbors that you're having a party and invite them if you think they'll mix.
- On the day be dressed and ready well ahead of your guests arriving.

Planning food

Don't underestimate the importance of having the right kind of catering. Food can make or break a party, so give it plenty of thought—type, quantity and presentation—well in advance.

Where large numbers of people are standing around and, hopefully, mingling, the food should be evenly distributed throughout the party area, elegant, and bite-sized because guests will have a drink in one hand. You'll need a few willing helpers to do occasional rounds with the dishes and a pile of napkins.

It's nice to pace finger food, perhaps by starting off with cold snacks (crudités, tartlets, blinis, etc.) and moving onto hot, more filling bites (bruchetta, tempura, tiger shrimp, sausages, etc.). Keep to just one kind of canapé per serving plate for a better visual effect. Finish up with sweet items such as individual fruits dipped in chocolate or tiny tartlets. Serve the canapés on pretty plates, decorated with colorful but edible flowers such as pansies and rose petals, or resting on lush green leaves from your garden.

How much drink?

The right amount of wine or beer will help your party go with a swing, so work out how much to buy beforehand. It's always better to have too much than too little, and bear in mind that most retailers will allow you to return any unopened bottles. Amass an ample supply of glasses, too. Many will be discarded or broken. If you can, rent two to three times more glasses than the number of guests, unless you have someone lined up to wash and dry empties during the party.

Wine: allow at least half a standard bottle per person, ideally three-quarters, with roughly equal quantities of red and white; order about 30 percent more than you calculate you need to be on the safe side.

Spirits: allow one or two measures per person as aperitifs. A standard bottle normally gives 30 measures. Unless you're specifically having a cocktail party, you're better off sticking to wine and beer, perhaps with a couple of basics like rum and cola, vodka and orange juice, or gin and tonic for spirit aficionados.

Beer: a barbecue on a long, hot summer's day could see your thirsty guests downing several bottles each so be generous and order at least four bottles for every potential beer drinker.

Champagne: it's a nice idea to welcome guests with a glass of champagne or high-quality sparkling wine as they arrive. After the champagne you can move on to wine.

A GUIDE TO WINE
when to drink and how to serve it

	White Burgundy / White Chianti	Sherry	Sauternes	Port	Moselle	Madeira	Liqueurs	Hock Graves	Red Chianti / Claret	Champagne	Burgundy
Aperitifs		❖				❖				❖	
Soup		❖				❖					
Fish	❖				❖			❖		❖	
White Meat	❖		❖		❖			❖		❖	
Red Meat									❖		❖
Game									❖		❖
Sweets			❖							❖	
Fruits			❖								
After Meals		❖		❖		❖	❖				

THE RIGHT GLASS FOR THE RIGHT WINE

Left to right - liqueur, sherry, white wine, claret, Rhine wine, champagne, and brandy.

Wine glasses are designed to hold a certain amount of liquid: the capacity and shape vary with the type of wine.

Sherry, served in a small stemmed glass.

Claret, served in a tulip-shaped, stemmed glass, holding twice as much as a sherry glass.

White wine, served in a tulip-shaped, stemmed glass; in size this is roughly half-way between a sherry and a claret glass.

Rhine wine, served in a tall-stemmed glass with a round cup.

Champagne, served in a saucer-shaped glass on a tall stem.

Port, served in a small, tulip-shaped, stemmed glass, a little larger than a sherry glass.

Liqueurs, served in tiny, stemmed glasses or miniature tumblers.

Brandy, served in crystal, balloon-shaped glasses.

How to be Star of the Barbecue

On a warm summer's day what could be more pleasant than a relaxed barbecue with friends and family? There's an art to doing a good barbecue, though, and a little practice will help you to master it.

Keep it safe

- Always make sure that the barbecue is on a firm, heat-proof surface, well away from buildings, trees, fences, and flammable items.
- Never leave the barbecue unattended.
- Keep children and pets away from the barbecue area.
- Use only proper barbecue lighters. Never use paraffin, gasoline, mineral spirit, or lighter fuel to start the barbecue as they can cause flames to spurt dangerously.
- Use long-handled tongs and oven gloves to avoid burning yourself.

Top tips

- Make sure that your barbecue is large enough to accommodate the food you intend to cook for your guests.
- Light your barbecue around 45 minutes before you start cooking. The charcoal should be white-hot and smoldering rather than burning before you start. If you put the food on too early, it can catch fire and blacken.
- Prepare everything else as much as you can before you start cooking.
- Food stays fresher if it is kept inside until it is ready to be cooked or served. Keep prepared food covered where possible.
- Lightly brush the cooking rack with a little

oil to help prevent the food from sticking.
- Offer a few vegetarian alternatives. Try vegetable kebabs, using wooden skewers soaked in water for 30 minutes that help the vegetables to keep their shape.
- To prevent your food from becoming overcooked or burned on the outside, wrap it in foil as a protective barrier.
- Throw a handful of herbs on the charcoal to produce a Mediterranean-style aroma.
- Try to buy charcoal produced from sustainable sources. This reduces the demand for fuel made from tropical hardwoods.

chapter 9

Moving Home

A Successful Move

It's said that moving home is one of life's most stressful events, but with good forward planning you can contain the upheaval. Lists, lists, and more lists are the answer, plus a detailed schedule that ideally starts two months before the big day. Never assume that everyone involved in the move knows exactly what's going on—always doublecheck.

Tips for a stress-free move

Obtain an estimate: you will need two or three quotations because they can vary considerably. Be clear about what is going to move, and make sure that you include the contents of your garage, shed, or attic.

The date: arrange this as far ahead as possible and try not to move on a Friday, the busiest day of the week. You can save money by booking your move for midweek.

Utilities: your moving company may not be allowed to interfere with mains services, so make arrangements with gas, electricity, water boards, and plumbers well in advance.

Deep freezers: try to use up your food stocks before you move because they may not travel well and will be an extra worry.

Carpets/curtains: discuss whether you want your moving company to remove curtains, fitted carpets and blinds, and then install them in your new home.

System or self-assembly furniture: some kit or self-assembly furniture can be taken apart and then reassembled, but it probably won't go back together again as well as it did the first time. Talk this possibility through with your moving company.

Packing: you can save yourself a lot of hassle and leave it all to professionals, especially as anything you pack yourself will not be covered by insurance in most contracts. Small, valuable items such as jewelry are often not included in a moving company's insurance policy so carry them yourself. If you are concerned about valuable or fragile items such as pianos, plants, fine art, wine, or antiques, discuss them with the company in advance.

Insurance: accidents happen, so insure belongings that are being moved, either through your removals firm or through your usual household insurer—but check the small print for any exclusions and excesses.

Going Green

Don't just throw away all your unwanted stuff. Take it to a recycling center or give it to a worthy charity so that someone else can benefit from it.

The new home: give your moving company a map showing your new address and a contact telephone number. Pinpoint where you want your possessions in the new home. Drawing up a plan and using color-coded labels is helpful. You'll need to have someone reliable at the collection and delivery addresses to keep an eye on things.

Parking: ask your new neighbors to ensure adequate parking space for the removal vehicle. Warn your mover about any parking restrictions at either house. Restricted access or parking can increase the amount of time needed to load and unload the vehicle so you may end up paying a surcharge.

Apartments and flats: if the elevator is small—or if there isn't one—warn the moving company in advance to avoid delays and difficulties when the moving team arrives.

Unloading: warn your moving company about exceptional problems such as poor access, narrow doorways, or spiral staircases.

Spare key: waiting time may incur extra charges, so if you have a key to your new home, give it to the foreman when leaving your old one in case the removal van arrives before you do.

Children and pets: lock pets indoors, allocate someone to look after the children, or have children and pets looked after by relatives so you don't have to worry about them.

Mythbuster!

Moving to a new house doesn't have to be one of life's most stressful events. Plan it like a military operation, write lists for everything, and you'll sail through it.

Countdown to Moving

Start planning your move well in advance for peace of mind on the big day.

Two to four weeks before

■ **Removals:** when the moving consultant calls, be very clear about what is going and what is staying.

■ **Packing:** if you have decided to do this yourself, begin at least two weeks before your move. Label boxes with the details of their contents and the room in which they are to be placed at the new address. Pack heavy objects at the bottom of boxes with lighter ones on top. Don't be tempted to overfill boxes. Sort out clutter and sell unwanted items, or take them to charity stores.

■ **Carpets/curtains:** if you are ordering these for your new home, confirm the correct delivery dates.

■ **Pets:** make arrangements to book pets into kennels or for friends and relatives to look after them during the move.

■ **Change-of-address notification.** Organizations you will need to inform about your change of address include:

Bank
Credit/store-card companies
Schools
Tax offices
Savings accounts, stocks, and shares
Social services
Pension provider
Insurance firm
Driving license bureau
Doctor/dentist/optician
Post office
Telephone, mobile, e-mail and internet
   service providers
TV and cable services
Private medical-care provider
Clubs, charities, etc. (for subscriptions)
Printers for the printing of change-of-
   address cards

One week before the move

■ **Utilities:** contact gas, electricity, telephone, and water companies to arrange for disconnection and reconnection of supply.

■ **Library:** take all the books back that you have out on loan.

■ **Milk/newspapers:** settle outstanding accounts and cancel or move supplies.

Three days before the move

■ Pack a bag with a change of clothes and essential toiletries. It's handy to put together a portable "survival kit" with all the essentials you may need.

■ Do a last-minute laundry. If you're putting belongings into storage for a long time, sort out some clothes for next season.

■ Ensure that the keys for your new home are available.

Two days before the move

■ Empty, defrost, and dry out your fridge/freezer if you are planning to put it into storage for any period of time.

■ If you're moving your freezer with all of its

> ## The Household Genie's Tip
>
> Put together a survival kit containing light bulbs, toilet paper, candles, a screwdriver and pliers, matches, paper towels, soap, a change of clothes, snacks, cash, and a list of key telephone numbers. Don't forget it when you move!

contents over a short distance, place the contents in plastic bags so that they can be lifted out quickly to facilitate the movement of the freezer.

■ Seal packets, bottles, or jars with tape to prevent leaks.

■ Pack valuables and documents and put them in a safe place.

■ Organize parking if necessary and sort out elevator access in the case of apartments.

The day before the move

■ Arrange meals and snacks for the next day, but remember that your stove may already be disconnected. Pack basics such as tea and coffee, milk, juice cartons, cookies, fruit, cheese, and packaged snacks. Put aside disposable plates, cups, and cutlery.

■ Plan the evening meal for move day. It may be easier to eat in a restaurant.

■ Prepare plants for travel.

Moving day

■ Strip the beds. Keep linen, towels, a change of clothes, and essential toiletries in a box or sack that travels with you so it will be instantly available on the first night and the following morning.

■ Settle the children with their carer. If they are staying with you, organize a room with their toys and a few treats. Older children may want to help with specific tasks, like packing their personal box.

■ Show the moving-team leader around the house and explain how you have organized your boxes.

■ Offer the team soda or coffee and snacks to keep them refreshed.

■ Once the van has been loaded, walk around the house with the moving-team leader to ensure that all items to be moved have been placed in the vehicle.

■ At your new home, check that everything is unloaded and placed in the appropriate rooms and, if quoted for, unpacked and unwrapped by the moving team.

■ Once you are satisfied that everything has been delivered and positioned safely in the appropriate places, you will be asked to acknowledge this by signing the team leader's delivery sheet and writing down any comments you may wish to make.

Your Essential Checklist

Use this checklist to make sure that you've done everything you're supposed to do before your moving day.

- ☐ Confirm removal dates and moving company
- ☐ Sign and return contract together with payment
- ☐ Clear the attic
- ☐ Book insurance at declared value
- ☐ Organize parking at new home
- ☐ Arrange a contact number
- ☐ Plan where things go in new home
- ☐ Dispose of anything you don't want
- ☐ Cancel the milk/newspapers
- ☐ Start using up freezer contents
- ☐ Clean out the freezer
- ☐ Contact carpet fitters if needed
- ☐ Arrange for someone to look after children/pets
- ☐ Notify utilities for disconnections

- ☐ Find and label keys
- ☐ Cancel all rental agreements
- ☐ Notify doctor, dentist, optician, veterinarian
- ☐ Address cards to friends and relatives
- ☐ Tell your bank and saving/share accounts
- ☐ Separate trinkets, jewelry, and small items
- ☐ Inform telephone company
- ☐ Sort out linen and clothes
- ☐ Ask post office to reroute mail
- ☐ Put garage/garden tools together
- ☐ Tell car registration and passport offices
- ☐ Take down curtains/blinds
- ☐ Notify credit-card companies
- ☐ Collect children's toys
- ☐ Make local map to new house for friends
- ☐ Organize basic catering for family at new home

"How will I remember to do everything?"

Index

Picture Credits

All images below © Getty Images, Inc.

p. 6   Miserable Mrs Mop, circa 1945

p. 8   New Cooker, 1961

p. 11   Making Notes, circa 1955

p. 28   Dusting, 1954

p. 29   Happy Housewife, circa 1955

p. 33   Top Tip, 197

p. 35   A Lifeguard House, 1951

p. 61   The joy of Vim, 1951

p. 66   Happy Housewife, circa 1965

p. 73   Family Silver, 1968

p. 80   Lace Renaissance, 1960

p. 87   Walking The Dog, 1952

p. 90   A Cold Shower

p. 101   Jack Of All Trades, circa 1950

p. 10   Sore Finger, circa 1955

p. 103   Pills and Thrills, circa 1955

p. 107   Domestic Accident, 1956

p. 112, 118   Wash Day, 1956

p. 119   Clean And Fresh, 1951

p. 124   Every Little Helps

p. 127   50s Housewife, circa 1955

p. 128   Welcome Snack, circa 1965

p. 131   Party Hostess, 1955

p. 136   On The Phone, 1953

p. 3, 58, 70, and cover © Advertising Archive Ltd

p. 138   © H. Armstrong Roberts/CORBIS

p. 76   The Advertising Archive Ltd. / © SEPS:
Curtis Publishing, Indianapolis, IN.